The Liberating Gods

4/28/25

11904

The Liberating Gods

EMERSON ON POETS AND POETRY

BY JOHN Q. ANDERSON

UNIVERSITY OF MIAMI PRESS
Coral Gables, Florida

Designed by Mary Lipson

Manufactured in the United States of America

Appreciation is hereby expressed to the Faculty Research
Support Program of the University of Houston for a grant-in-aid
for completion of the manuscript.

In memory of
Ernest Allen Epps, Sr.,
who loved Emerson

Contents

The Liberating Gods

. . . we love the poet. . . . He unlocks our chains and admits us to a new scene.

The poet . . . will tell us how it was with him, and all men will be the richer in his fortune.

The use of symbols has a certain power of emancipation and exhilaration for all men. We seem to be touched by a wand which makes us dance, and run about happily, like children. . . . This is the effect on us of tropes, fables, oracles and all poetic forms. Poets are thus liberating gods.

Introduction

EMERSON WAS OFTEN unhappy with literary criticism and critics of his time, as indicated by comments scattered throughout his works. Criticism was "infested with a cant of materialism," he charged, and was "timid"; therefore, "the critic destroys" and is "a failed poet." While finishing "The Poet," his major essay about poets and poetry, Emerson facetiously wrote to Christopher P. Cranch, "I am a vigorous, cruel critic, and demand in the poet a devotion that seems hardly possible in our hasty, facile America." [1] Then, in that essay he declared that he was not "wise enough" to be a critic (*Works*, III, 38).[2]

Several twentieth-century commentators have refused to accept Emerson's disavowal of the role of critic. From Norman Foerster in 1928 to Therman O'Daniel in 1964,[3] critics have complained about Emerson's "transcendental" criticism, but they have generally agreed that his concepts are too important in the history of literary criticism to be ignored.

Though Emerson was interested in all forms of literature, he was most concerned with poetry. In the late 1830's he developed an interest in the criticism of poetry. All along he had read Plato in whom he found comments on poetic inspiration and the treatment of subject matter in poetry. In Thomas Taylor's translations of Plato and the Neo-Platonic commentary Taylor appended, Emerson found much discussion of the divine origin of poetry and its relation to intuition and inspiration.[4] Emerson was familiar with Aristotle's *Poetics* and twice noted in his *Journals* that "Poetry is something more philosophical and excellent than history" (*Journals*, II, 440; IX, 296).[5] He read the miscellaneous works of Sidney, probably including the *Defence of Poesie*, and he knew the commentary on poetry of Jonson, Dryden, Pope, and Coleridge.[6] Early in his career he mentions Wordsworth's theory and practice of poetry, which he gradually understood and finally commended, and he read Shelley's *Defence of Poetry* soon after it was published in 1840. By 1841, Emerson was ready to offer his opinions publicly and included a lecture entitled "The Poet" in a series given in Boston in the winter of that year. He wrote to Margaret Fuller in 1842 that he had been reading on "the subject of poetry," [7] which may indicate that he was then forming his major pronouncement on the topic, the essay "The Poet," published as the first of *Essays: Second Series* in 1844. In the years following other pieces on poets and poetry appeared—the essay on Shakespeare in *Representative Men*, two essays on Milton, the essays "Poetry and Imagination" and "Art and Criticism," and many entries in the *Journals*. He also continued to write poems that are concerned with poetry. Near the end of his life, he gathered together his favorite poems in *Parnassus*.[8]

Emerson's preoccupation with poetry was the result of his conviction that he himself was a poet—in the broadest sense of that word. In a letter to his wife Lidian in 1835 he wrote, "I am born a poet, of a low class without doubt yet a poet." He continued, "That is my nature and vocation. My singing to be sure is very 'husky' and is for the most part in prose. Still I am a poet in the sense of a perceiver & dear lover of the harmonies that are in the soul & in matter, and specially of the correspondence between these & those" (*Letters*, I, 435).

Emerson thought of himself as a poet in the way he understood the Neo-Platonists' designation of Plato as the first poet and in the way that he himself thought of Thomas Taylor, the great commentator on Plato, as a poet. Emerson may have realized by 1835 that his role was not that of the creator of great poems in the manner of Milton and Shakespeare, whom he so revered. If he were not, then, to sing in meter and rhyme, he might well in his "husky" voice chaunt in musical prose as Plato had done. Thus, as "a perceiver & dear lover of the harmonies of the universe," he might well become a "feeder" of poets, as he said Taylor was (*Works*, VIII, 50). If he could not command the whole of nature and the world of men as symbols of his thought as he felt that Shakespeare had done, he might show "the virtue which resides in these symbols" as he said Shakespeare had not done. If he could not justify the ways of God to man in nineteenth-century America as he felt that Milton had done for his time, perhaps he could incite some younger American poet with a less husky voice to do just that without being "too literary," as he thought Milton had been. If he could not himself translate the divine fury into "bardic sentences" that could "transfix the land and the sea," then he could display the "lustres" he had garnered from East and West so that they might outshine the fool's gold of American materialism and thereby illumine man in this new world. If he could not, like his beloved Saadi, write a stanza of poetry so pleasing to God that a host of angels would descend with "salvers of glory," then he could man the watchtower and hail from afar those new poets, "the liberating gods," that were sure to come to sing of the new nation, for "America is a poem . . . and it will not wait long for metres" (*Works*, III, 38).

While he waited, Emerson did not despair that such "liberating gods" did not immediately appear. Instead, he was busy in his own way—enlarging the concept of the nature of the poet, broadening the function of the poet in society, calling for greater freedom of choice of subject matter for the poet, and phrasing a fuller statement of ideals for American poetry. And he continued to write poems that reflect his vision. It may yet be recognized that his was the dual role he described in his *Journals* (VII, 240): "The Poet is the lover loving; the critic is the lover advised."

CHAPTER ONE

The Nature of the Poet

EMERSON HAD A GREAT deal to say about the nature of the poet, and a consistent pattern of thought on the topic is discernible in the *Journals* and essays. The four main phases of this pattern are stated in the essay "The Poet": the poet is a representative man, he is endowed with superior intellectual perception, he is a seer and prophet, and he is the "Namer" and "Language-maker." These key points set forth in 1844 were amplified in other essays and in journal entries and sometimes illustrated in Emerson's poems.

The poet is a representative man, Emerson says in the essay "The Poet," because he "stands among partial men for the complete man, and apprises us not of his wealth, but of the common wealth" (*Works*, III, 5). Emerson's meaning is demonstrated in his *Representative Men*. For that volume, Emerson selected from the past various great men to illustrate the several divisions of human knowledge and accomplishment: Plato is the Philosopher; Swedenborg, the Mystic; Shakespeare, the Poet; and so on. The introductory essay, "Uses of Great Men," explains that each of these historical individuals reflects latent potentialities in the mind of every man; that is, every human being is something of a philosopher, a mystic, and a poet, although none of these attributes are as highly developed in him as they are in Plato, Swedenborg, and Shakespeare. Great men, Emerson concludes, are the "lenses through which we read our own minds" (*Works*, IV, 5). It follows then that the ordinary man has potentialities within his own soul, although circumstances have prevented his full development of them; even so, the ordinary man should not be intimidated by those who have fulfilled their potential.

The representative man is a type at the same time that he is a highly developed individual. For example, Emerson chooses Shakespeare as a representative man because he has "a heart in unison with his time and country" (*Works*, IV, 189), so that he is able to speak for his countrymen. At the same time, Shakespeare is the individual par excellence and is representative of the idea of poet. Great as Shakespeare is, he is still "the most indebted man" (*Works*, IV, 189).[1] He could not have been the genius that he was without the influence of his time: "Great genial power," Emerson observes, "one would almost say, consists in not being original at all; in being altogether receptive; in letting the world do all, and suffering the spirit of the hour to pass unobstructed through the mind" (*Works*, IV, 191). But Emerson, the apostle of individualism, would not concede that the time alone in which a man lives makes him great; the true poet remains an individual—perhaps the most individualistic of all men—despite the molding influence of his age. The very individualism of the poet and the nature of his art, in fact, tend to separate him from his time. Speaking of his own experience, Emerson says in the poem "The Apology":

> Think me not unkind and rude
> That I walk alone in grove and glen;
> I go to the god of the wood
> To fetch his word to men (*Works*, IX, 119).[2]

In the essay "The Poet," Emerson says that the poet "is isolated among his contemporaries by truth and by his art, but with this consolation in his pursuits, that they will draw all men sooner or later" (*Works*, III, 5). The withdrawal of the poet from his fellows is only intermittent; he remains the representative man.

Emerson's concept of Man Thinking in his essay, "The American Scholar" sheds further light on the representative role of the poet. Whereas the scholar is Man Thinking, the poet is Man Thinking and also Man Speaking in that he is capable of giving expression to his thoughts in the most compelling language. Ideally, Emerson maintains, "Every man should be so much an artist that he could report in conversation what had befallen him" (*Works*, III, 6), as the great poets can do. But practically speaking, most men are incapable of this comprehensive expression; consequently, the poet is necessary to men, because he is able to utter for them those thoughts which they, being less gifted, are unable to put into words. "The man is only half himself," Emerson asserts, "the other half is his expression" (*Works*, III, 5). The poet has power over the obstructions to this necessary expression: "The poet is the person in whom these powers are in balance, the man without impediment, who sees and handles that which others dream of, traverses the whole scale of experience, and is representative of man, in virtue of being the largest power to receive and impart" (*Works*, III, 6). This extraordinary power of expression coupled with the representative character of the poet indeed makes him stand for "the complete man" among "partial men."

What Emerson means by "the complete man" is made clear by reference to the Neo-Platonic concept that the soul contains all knowledge. The degree of completeness of the individual depends upon his recognition of the omniscience of the soul and his ability to utilize this knowledge. Emerson calls that man complete whose mental and spiritual powers are so well developed that he is able to employ to the fullest the potentialities of his soul.[3] Ideally, such an individual reflects the sum of all phases of human knowledge and action; he incorporates all the qualities of genius discussed in *Representative Men*. That such a man had ever existed, Emerson did not assume. Even Shakespeare, whom Emerson honored by making him representative of man as poet, was but a "half man"—a statement that has distressed those commentators who have not realized that the complete man of whom Emerson speaks, is, after all, an ...l.[4] Emerson does not, however, rule out the possibility that ... "complete" man *might* sometime exist. Fearful of the ex... of idealism, Emerson states that the poet *stands for* the com... , not that he *is* that ideal, although the "true" poet whom ...continued to seek certainly approaches that ideal, as ...did.

...re of the poet's worth as a representative man and of

the virtue which elevates him above ordinary men is his ability to
say for them what they cannot say for themselves; it is his nature
to do so, just as it is the nature of the great leaders of men, such as
Napoleon, to inspire them to great physical action. "Shakespeare's
principal merit," Emerson maintains, "may be conveyed in saying
that he of all men best understands the English language, and can
say what he will" (*Works*, IV, 15). Certainly, then, Shakespeare is
a true poet, if not the ideal, for he is "the man without impediment"
and "is representative of man."

Another aspect of Emerson's concept of the degree of completeness and of the representative nature of the poet is revealed in "The
Poet" in a myth of the kind used by Plato:

> For the Universe has three children, born at one time, which re-
> appear under different names in every system of thought, whether
> they be called cause, operation and effect; or, more poetically,
> Jove, Pluto, Neptune; or, theologically, the Father, the Spirit and
> the Son; but which we will call here the Knower, the Doer and
> the Sayer. These stand respectively for the love of truth, for the
> love of good, and for the love of beauty. These three are equal.
> Each is that which he is, essentially, so that he cannot be sur-
> mounted or analyzed, and each of these three has the power of the
> others latent in him and his own, patent (*Works*, III, 6–7).

In this myth, with its Proclean image of the triad,[5] the poet is
mythologically Neptune, theologically, the Son, and intellectually,
the Sayer. The triad becomes the monad, and thus esthetically the
poet is the lover of beauty. To the original mythological concept
of Neptune as ruler of the sea, Proclus adds the idea of Neptune's
being symbolic of power; Emerson, following Proclus probably,
equates the poet with Neptune and so implies that the poet represents power of the mind as well as power over mind. Emerson also
indicates that in equating the poet with the Son, the poet is the
vital link between the physical and the spiritual, with overtone
meaning involving sacrifice, humility, and passion. In equatin
poet with the Sayer, Emerson emphasizes the poet as the *va*
man who has "the largest power to receive and to impart"
truths. These characteristics combined, then, make th
lover of beauty, for that is what he seeks to create. Si
"man of Beauty," he, by his very nature, recognizes th

cept of beauty inhere the ideas of unity, form, vitality, reconciliation of opposites, and the creative impulse itself.[6] "For the world,"
Emerson states, "is not painted or adorned, but is from the beginning beautiful. . . . Beauty is the creator of the universe" (*Works*,
III, 7). The poet as the man of beauty has as his primary aim the
seeking, isolating, and explaining of that almost inexplicable quality
of the triad "the eternal trinity of Truth, Goodness, and Beauty"
which Emerson mentions in the essay "The Transcendentalist"
(*Works*, I, 354). In that piece, Emerson says that the transcendentalist prefers to make "Beauty the sign and head" of this trinity,
and Emerson himself is tempted to do likewise. For instance, in his
poem "Ode to Beauty" (*Works*, IX, 87–90), he describes himself
as the "credulous lover" whose heart Beauty long ago stole but
whom he has never been able to capture. The "dangerous glances"
of Beauty "Make women of men"; this Beauty, glimpsed everywhere in nature, is always "gliding through the sea of forms,"
never to be possessed. He concludes that he "dare not die" "Lest
there I find the same deceiver / And be the sport of Fate forever."
He pleads with Beauty, "Dread Power, but dear! if God thou be, /
Unmake me quite, or give thyself to me!"

Less passionately, in the essay "Beauty," Emerson says, "I am
warned by the ill fate of many philosophers not to attempt a definition of Beauty. I will rather enumerate a few of its qualities. We
ascribe beauty to that which is simple; which has no superfluous
parts; which exactly answers its end; which stands related to all
things; which is the mean of many extremes. It is the most enduring
quality, and the most ascending quality" (*Works*, VI, 289). The
poet, as the man of Beauty, by nature is concerned with the "most
enduring quality," and, ideally, if he creates that same beauty of
which he himself is a part, his work rises above other forms of expression—philosophy, for example. Or rather, the poet as the man
of Beauty with the powers of the Knower and Doer latent in him
in a sense rises above them in creating that beauty which reflects
Beauty as "the creator of the Universe."

Recognition of his role as creator and man of Beauty leads the
poet to another important power of the soul—complete faith in the
divine origin, creation, and purpose of man and his world. Such a
faith does not depend on man-made authority or dogma; rather it

depends on knowledge of the harmonious interdependence within
the universe, perceived and verified within his own soul. This faith
permits no doubt, despite the conflicting testimony of the senses,
and it gives the poet what Emerson calls "a centred mind" (*Works*,
III, 19). Such a mind, relying on intuition, looks out from the center of the individual, who is the microcosm of the universe, and
sees the whole circle of God, man, and nature, and intuitively perceives the underlying unity in creation. This perception of absolute unity was "the lapse" of Uriel in Emerson's poem of that name.
"With a look that [dis]solved the sphere," Uriel saw that

> 'Line in nature is not found;
> Unit and universe are round;
> In vain produced, all rays return;
> Evil will bless, and ice will burn' (*Works*, IX, 14).

Since the poet utilizes the power of "the centred mind," he is no
"permissive potentate, but is emperor in his own right. . . . He is a
sovereign, and stands on the centre" (*Works*, III, 7).[7] Such is Emerson's "kingly bard" Merlin in the poem of that name (*Works*, IX,
120–124).

After Emerson had established the representative character of
the poet, he proceeded to add the second trait, "ulterior intellectual
perception," whereby the poet "stands one step nearer to things,
and sees the flowing or metamorphosis" (*Works*, III, 20). The innate insight of the poet is superior, Emerson argues, to that of ordinary men, though they share to some degree in this intuition. A
journal passage explains this special kind of seeing:

> . . . every man may be, and some men are, raised to a platform
> whence he sees beyond sense to moral and spiritual truth; when
> he no longer sees snow as snow, or horses as horses, but only sees
> or names them representatively for those interior facts which
> they signify. This is the way the poets use them. And in that
> exalted state, the mind deals very easily with great and small
> material things, and strings worlds, like beads upon its thought
> (*Journals*, VIII, 520–521).

In the poem "The Poet" the poet's "solar eyes"

> Saw the endless rack of the firmament...
> And through man and woman and sea and star
> Saw the dance of Nature forward and far,
> Through worlds and races and terms and times
> Saw musical order and pairing rhymes (*Works*, IX, 311).[8]

The poet's mind, aware of its "ulterior intellectual perception," remains in a kind of alerted state of suspended receptivity. Accustomed as it is to dealing with intangibles, it is always ready to entertain intimations of truth which lie seemingly beyond the limits of provable knowledge and is able to understand them at once. To some degree the poet may induce these flights by contemplation. The poet "resigns himself to his mood, and that thought which agitated him is expressed ... in a manner totally new" (*Works*, III, 24). Through the intuition, "He is a beholder of ideas and an utterer of the necessary and casual" (*Works*, III, 8), because he has penetrated "into that region where the air is music," where he hears "those primal warblings," audible only to "men of more delicate ear" (*Works*, III, 8).

But the intuition, important as it is to the "ulterior intellectual perception," is of ultimate value only when the truth which it perceives finds expression in recognizable form. Hence, a transference from the spiritual form or mental image to the physical form or an object of art is necessary. This transference may be immediate, or it may, on the other hand, be a slow process. From his own experience, Emerson knew how difficult it was to translate the vision to a poem, as a journal entry shows:

> I go discontented thro' the world
> Because I cannot strike
> The harp to please my tyrannous ear:
> Gentle touches are not wanted. . . .

He wanted his lines to be "strokes of fate" (as his Merlin's were) that would capture the "ample winds," "the pulse of human blood," and "the voice of mighty men." The fragment concludes:

> I will not read a pretty tale
> To pretty people in a nice saloon
> Borrowed from their expectation,

But I will sing aloud and free
From the heart of the world (*Works*, IX, 441).

The transference from vision to poem is made possible by the aid of inspiration, the active agent of the intuition. Emerson maintains that the success with which a poet is able to deal with intuitively perceived truths and to transfer them to forms recognizable by other men depends upon the strength of his inspiration. In the essay "Inspiration," he explains:

> The poet cannot see a natural phenomenon which does not express to him a correspondent fact in his mental experience; he is made aware of a power to carry on and complete the metamorphosis of natural into spiritual facts. Everything which we hear for the first time was expected by the mind; the newest discovery was expected. In the mind we call this enlarged power Inspiration. I believe that nothing great and lasting can be done except by inspiration, by leaning on the secret augury (*Works*, VIII, 271).

This deep and abiding faith in inspiration never altered throughout Emerson's life. The preface to his collection of favorite poems, *Parnassus*, composed when he was past seventy, differentiates between "poets by education and practice" and "poets by nature"— that is, by inspiration. Pope, he says, was the best example of the poet by education and practice; Milton, too, had educational advantages, "but was also poet born." Chaucer, Shakespeare, Jonson ("despite all the pedantic lumber he dragged with him"), Herbert, Herrick, Collins, Burns, and Wordsworth were poets by nature, and "these we love" (*Parnassus*, Preface, p. iv). The poet by nature, Emerson believes, relies on the mystical powers of intuition and inspiration; therefore, he has "ulterior intellectual perception." The poet by education and practice produces poetry that is technically correct but lacks the inner fire, a sign of genuine inspiration.

In addition to intuition and inspiration, imagination is an essential part of the poet's "ulterior intellectual perception." Imagination is that quality of mind which enables the poet to give form to the truths which he perceives intuitively. In "The Poet" Emerson explains that the poet's insight expresses itself in "what is called Imagination . . . a very high sort of seeing, which does not come by study, but by the intellect being where and what it sees" (*Works*, III, 26). He goes on to say that the intellectual man knows that beyond the energy of expression of which he is conscious there is a new energy which he can reach only by abandoning himself to spiritual power. This power, not unlike that described in "The Over-Soul,"

> is a great public power on which he can draw, by unlocking, at all risks, his human doors, and suffering the ethereal tides to roll and circulate through him; then he is caught up into the life of the Universe, his speech is thunder, his thought is law, and his words are universally intelligible as the plants and animals (*Works*, III, 26–27).

It is this quality of imagination by which the poet is able to project his mind beyond the bounds of generally accepted rationality. As Emerson further describes this process:

> The poet knows that he speaks adequately then only when he speaks somewhat wildly, or 'with the flower of the mind'; not with the intellect used as an organ, but with the intellect released from all service and suffered to take its direction from its celestial life; or as the ancients were wont to express themselves, not with the intellect alone but with the intellect inebriated by nectar (*Works*, III, 27).

This inebriation of the intellect is akin to Wordsworth's mystical experience described in "Tintern Abbey," in which a sensory perception passes first into the heart to become a moral sense, and eventually into the soul with such force that the original sensory experience is lost and the body is "laid asleep." It is this same quality of imagination of which Wordsworth speaks when he says that the poet may "for short spaces of time ... slip into an entire delusion, and even confound and identify his own feelings" with those of other men.[9] Emerson's Saadi experienced this same transport:

> He stood before the tumbling main
> With joy too tense for sober brain;
> He shared the life of the element,
> The tie of blood and home was rent:
> As if in him the welkin walked,

> The winds took flesh, the mountains talked,
> And he the bard, a crystal soul
> Sphered and concentric with the whole (*Works*, IX, 322).

This "ulterior intellectual perception" enables the poet to see through the "flowing vest" of the physical world and to understand the unity within the universe; by its help he "turns the world to glass, and shows us all things in their right series and procession" (*Works*, III, 20). Such perception, moreover, enables him to see the "flowing or metamorphosis" of forms, both physical and spiritual, so that he does not confuse appearances with realities.[10]

Because the poet naturally perceives the organic nature of the universe and understands the constant flux of things, he is the greatest of scientists, according to Emerson (*Works*, III, 21). Evidently he means that the poet's more extensive experience in spiritual matters and his ability to see the analogy between physical and spiritual laws enable him to understand the organization of the universe better than the scientist who is trained to view only a small part of the physical world. The poet is a specialist "in universes," as it were; unlike the scientist who may, for example, study leaf, branch, and flower and see the unity therein, the poet goes further and sees that the unity that the living organism displays symbolizes the simplicity and unity of spiritual laws. The poet sees, as the scientist does not, that the plant is symbolic of the unity of soul and universe: "The Universe is the externization of the soul. Wherever the life is, that bursts into appearance around it" (*Works*, III, 14). The scientist refuses to take this extrarational leap; hence, "Our science is sensual, and therefore superficial," Emerson concludes. "The earth and the heavenly bodies, physics and chemistry, we sensually treat, as if they were self-existent but these are the retinue of that Being we have" (*Works*, III, 14). Emerson continues by quoting Proclus to the effect that the heavens themselves exhibit images of intellectual perception.

Emerson was not antagonistic to science. On the contrary, he shared the friendly attitude toward scientific investigation common with other writers of the early nineteenth century—Wordsworth, for instance[11]—and was interested in scientific reports, although he read them more for "lustres" (their suggestive value) than for specific information.[12] His real interest in botany lay in his conviction that elements of nature were symbolic of spiritual forms and laws which exceeded them in perfection and beauty. Like the poet whom he describes, Emerson takes an expansive view, as shown in this passage in the *Journals*:

> The poet, the true naturalist, for example, domesticates himself in nature with a sense of strict consanguinity. His own blood is in the rose and apple-tree. The Cause of him is Cause of all. The volcano has its analogies in him. He is in the chain of magnetic, electric, geologic, meteorologic phenomena, and so he comes to live in nature and extend his being through all: then is true science (*Journals*, V, 179).

By fuller utilization of the powers of the soul and by "ulterior intellectual perception," the poet displays his third major capability—seer and prophet.

In designating the poet as seer and prophet, Emerson was, as he knew, following a long line of theorizers. Plato, for instance, assumes that poets as well as philosophers have access to permanent truths beyond the reach of sensory experience. Aristotle "does not altogether ignore the 'transport' of poetry"[13] and he implies qualities of mind of the seer and prophet in the poet. In his defense of poetry, Sidney places the poet in the exalted position of seer and prophet.[14] Shelley notes that from ancient times poets were called "legislators, or prophets" who see "the future in the present."[15] In Carlyle, however, Emerson found the most explicit statement of the role of the poet as seer and prophet.

> The true Poet is ever, as of old [Carlyle says], the Seer; whose eye has been gifted to discern the godlike Mystery of God's Universe, and decipher some new lines of its celestial writing; we can still call him a *Vates* and Seer; for he *sees* into this greatest of secrets, 'the open secret'; hidden things become clear; how the Future (both resting on Eternity) is but another phasis of the Present: Thereby are his words in very truth prophetic; what he has spoken shall be done.[16]

In his fable of the children of the universe in "The Poet," Emerson gives the Knower, the Doer, and the Sayer equal status, but the

Sayer is given the additional ability to write down in immortal language the permanent truths he perceives. The Knower and the Doer may also be seers, but they are not necessarily prophets, since they may not be able to make their discoveries known to man and certainly not in the same attractive way the poet does. This facility of expression gives the poet an edge over the man of reflection and the man of action.

Emerson's poet as seer, like Plato's philosopher, perceives the universals behind the particulars; he sees the unity in variety; he sees through external appearances into the eternal truths. In a world characterized by flux, the appearance of things may change but the truths behind things never alter. The capacity to penetrate the "flowing vest" is illustrated in Emerson's poem "Woodnotes" in which the Muse instructs the poet that

> The rushing metamorphosis
> Dissolving all that fixture is,
> Melts things that be to things that seem,
> And solid nature to a dream (*Works*, IX, 52).
>
> All the forms are fugitive,
> But the substances survive (*Works*, IX, 57).

The poet has the ability to *see* into the very heart of reality and to record the results of such extraordinary vision in songs of beauty which reflect the interior truths perceived. This is indeed seeing "the open secret" and thereby turning "the world to glass" so that its beauty becomes evident to man.

"It was always the theory of literature," Emerson says, "that the word of a poet was authoritative and final" (*Works*, I, 211). In the role of prophet, the poet "announces that which no man foretold" (*Works*, III, 8). Emerson's own Merlin, the "kingly bard," creates a rhyme that "Modulates the king's affairs" (*Works*, IX, 120, 123). This "authority" comes by intuition in moments of inspiration. "The poet works to an end above his will," Emerson asserts, "and by means, too, which are out of his will" (*Works*, XII, 71). The poet resembles the Greek oracle who falls under the sway of power beyond control and becomes the voice of that mysterious power. The poet temporarily abandons himself to the overwhelming inspiration so that the "celestial currents" of spirit flow through him and he speaks for the spirit. The relationship of this ecstatic state to Plato's "divine fury" is obvious.[17] In addition, it is not unlike the state of exaltation described by mystics as the "mystical union." Yet Emerson's poet, never, it seems, becomes so completely will-less in his oracular moods as the mystic who in the trance-like state verges on the loss of self. Although the poet also seeks an interfusion of spirit, he does not desire the complete loss of identity in spirit which renders his mental faculties passive and prevents his creative imagination from recreating the experience for other men. Emerson, in fact, warns at least once against intoxication; in the poem "The Poet" Emerson says:

> His learning should be deep and large,
> And his training should not scant
> The deepest lore of wealth or want:
> His flesh should feel, his eyes should read
> Every maxim of dreadful Need;
> In its fulness he should taste
> Life's honeycomb, but not too fast;
> Full fed, but not intoxicated; (*Works*, IX, 310).

Emerson was concerned also with the manifestation of the prophetic power of the poet. Both Shelley and Carlyle had assigned to the poet the power of foretelling the future in light of the past and present. Emerson agrees when he says that the poet "announces that which no man foretold." In view of his belief that miracles are a matter of time rather than power,[18] this prophesying is based on knowledge of natural and spiritual laws rather than any magical suspension of law. Since the poet is aware of the inviolable laws which govern matter and spirit, he perceives the inevitable changes and announces them before they are seen by other men; hence, he is a prophet, for, as Emerson says, "he was present and privy to the appearance which he describes" (*Works*, III, 8).

As a seer, then, the poet perceives the truth, and as the *vates* he makes the truth known to other men. Or, as Coleridge says, he makes "the external internal, and the internal external." [19] The poet does not hoard his apperceptions as some mystics do; he must tell men "how it is with him" so that they may know how it might be with them. Emerson's Saadi, who by choice may sit with lords or churls, "his runes he rightly read, / And to his folk his message sped" (*Works*, IX, 132). The poet, Emerson declares, "Against all the appearance . . . sees and reports the truth." Consequently, his poetry is "the only verity,—the expression of a sound mind speaking after the ideal, and not after the apparent" (*Works*, VIII, 26–27).

The final attribute of the poet Emerson discusses in the essay "The Poet" is "Naming." This "expression or naming," Emerson contends, "is not art, but a second nature" (*Works*, III, 22). The poet puts the world "under the mind for verb and noun" and is the one "who can articulate it" (*Works*, III, 20).

The concept of the poet as "Namer" is, of course, an ancient idea. Emerson had read Thomas Taylor's paraphrase of Proclus with reference to Plato's *Cratylus* in which the twofold process of naming is discussed.[20] Taylor quotes Proclus as saying that names are "two-fold, one kind belonging to things perceptual, which are established according to science, and another to things corruptable, and which are subjects of doubt." Emerson echoes these ideas in "The Poet":

> . . . the poet is the Namer or Language-maker, naming things sometimes after their appearance, sometimes after their essence, and giving to every one its own name and not another's, thereby rejoicing the intellect, which delights in detachment or boundary (*Works*, III, 21).

Emerson assumes, moreover, that "The poets made all the words," that "each word was at first a stroke of genius," and that "Language is fossil poetry" (*Works*, III, 21–22).

This discussion of the poetic origin of language reflects Emerson's earlier contention in *Nature* that "Words are signs of natural facts" (*Works*, I, 25) and that words are now used to convey states of mind whereas originally they described material appearances. He assumes that language in "its infancy" was "all poetry," because it was so fresh and new that natural symbols served directly for spiritual facts. Presumably, all men were poets then. In latter times, poets alone retain this pristine ability to give names and create words that are symbolic of natural facts. This attribute of the poet explains the power of poetry over the minds of men.

Since poets made the words, it is natural that they should use them with more facility and more effectively than other men. In a journal entry, Emerson explains:

> ... the poet goes straight forward to say his thought, and the words and images fly to him to express it, whilst cooler moods are forced to hint the matter, or insinuate, or perhaps only allude to it, being unable to fuse and mould their words and images to fluid obedience (*Journals*, IX, 312).

Nor is this ability entirely an ideal; there had been poets, Emerson believes, who were Namers and Language-makers in this sense. Shakespeare, Milton, and sometimes Wordsworth had these qualities. With Shakespeare, for example, "Poetry," Emerson says, "is no verbal affair; the thought is poetical, and Nature is put under contribution to give analogies and semblances that she has never yielded before" (*Journals*, III, 290). Milton "was a benefactor of the English Tongue," and a description of his poetry requires "words implying, not creation, but increased perception, second-sight knowledge of what *is*, beyond the ken of others" (*Journals*, II, 364). In his essay on Milton in the *North American Review* (1838), Emerson observes:

> His mastery of his native tongue was more than to use it as well as any other; he cast it into new forms. He uttered in it things unheard before. Not imitating but rivalling Shakspeare, he scattered, in tones of prolonged and delicate melody, his pastoral and romantic fancies; then, soaring into unattempted strains, he made it capable of an unknown majesty, and bent it to express every trait of beauty, every shade of thought ... (*Works*, XII, 260–261).

At times Emerson indicates that the attribute of naming in the poet is mystical, somewhat like the prophetic ability which has already been noted. The strong stimuli of inspiration may cause the imagination of the poet to range far beyond the limits of sensory perception in quest of final meanings. In "Poetry and Imagination," Emerson discusses this transcendence:

> The poet is enamoured of thoughts and laws. These know their way, and guided by them, he is ascending from an interest in

visible things to an interest in that which they signify, and from the part of a spectator to the part of a maker. And as everything streams and advances, as every faculty and every desire is pro-creant, and every perception is a destiny, there is no limit to his hope (*Works*, VIII, 42).

In his poem "The Poet" Emerson's poet as namer

Threw to each fact a tuneful name.
The things whereon he cast his eyes
Could not the nations rebaptize,
Nor Time's snows hide the names he set,
Nor last posterity forget (*Works*, IX, 309).

The attribute of Namer and Language-maker, when added to the attributes of Sayer, seer, and prophet, makes the poet indeed "the man without impediment."

Emerson's concept of the nature of the poet reflects his natural eclecticism. He blends elements of the philosophy of Idealism, Neo-Platonic concepts and terminology, and Transcendental dogmas with ideas from the historical commentary on poetry, particularly the innate nobility of the poet and the capacity of poetry to express the most profound truths. These hospitable ideas are fused with his own bedrock belief in self-sufficient individualism.

Despite his exalted status, Emerson's poet is no mystic or recluse; he does not forget less gifted men, for he is their representative and he must live in their world at the same time that he shows them the beauty of the world beyond. This tension between the world of ideas and the world of men Emerson illustrates in his own poetry through his Merlin and Saadi. Merlin represents the uncompromis-ing ideal in its magnificence, grandeur, and austere splendor; the kingly bard Merlin smites "the chords rudely and hard / As with hammer or with mace," and his imperious tones strike awe in the hearts of his listeners—awe, not so much of him as of the over-powering truths he utters. By contrast, gentle Saadi, no less divine than Merlin, passes unobtrusively through the halls of the great and the huts of the poor, and the "Sunshine in his heart" makes "each transparent word" he utters another strand in the graceful net of love in which he holds the race of men.

CHAPTER TWO

The Function of the Poet

THE FUNCTION OF THE POET in society is determined by his nature as a representative man. As Sayer, seer, and prophet he speaks for other men as a wise legislator speaks for his constituents. Such an analogy was natural to Emerson who saw correspondences all around him:

> Everything should be treated poetically,—law, politics, house-keeping, money. A judge and a banker must drive their craft poetically as well as a dancer or a scribe. That is, they must exert that higher vision which causes the object to become fluid and plastic. Then they are inventive, they detect its capabilities (*Journals*, V, 358).

If "spiritually" or "imaginatively" is substituted for "poetically" in the foregoing statement, it is clear that Emerson means that man's endeavors, whatever they may be, can reflect his own divinity and can be as a result dignified and worthwhile. The representative function of the poet enables him to show these lawyers, bankers, and politicians that it is possible to "drive their craft" with spiritual purpose. The poet has been "elected" to carry on their poetic business, just as they on a lower level make his laws, handle his money, and conduct his government. The poet's nature enables him to see clearly this position of his between the world of everyday affairs and the world of the spirit. Emerson states this relationship in this utilitarian image: "The poet, like the electric rod, must reach from a point nearer the sky than all surrounding objects, down to the earth, and into the dark wet soil, or neither is of use" (*Works*, XII, 366). More poetically, the idea is stated in the poem "Saadi":

> Yet Saadi loved the race of men,—
> No churl, immured in cave or den;
> In bower and hall
> He wants them all,
> Nor can dispense
> With Persia for his audience ... (*Works*, IX, 130).

Statements in the essay "The Poet," supplemented by remarks in other essays and the *Journals*, reveal three aspects of the function of the poet: he creates the great poetry of his nation in which he memorializes great men; he discloses the underlying unity in the universe between God, man, and nature and its benefits to man; and he acts as the "liberating god" who frees men from the prison of their everyday thoughts by bringing them glimpses of the higher realm of spirit.

Emerson says that a major function of the poet is "to create the songs of his nation" and thereby to immortalize its great men:

> The poet does not wait for the hero or the sage, but, as they act and think primarily, so he writes primarily what will and must be spoken, reckoning the others, though primaries also, yet, in respect to him, secondaries and servants; as sitters or models in the studio of a painter, or as assistants who bring building-materials to an architect (*Works*, III, 7–8).

Though Emerson places the poet as Sayer on an equal basis with the Knower (the sage) and the Doer (the hero), the poet has the advantage of unimpeded expression by which he can translate the profound thoughts of the philosopher and the virtuous acts of the hero into the language of men. Thus, heroes and sages become vehicles to body forth his thought. Also, the poet may create fictitious heroes and sages who may become as famous as any real men, if not more so. Men recognize the representative nature of the poet's creations and adopt them as truthful pictures of the thought and deeds of their own age and nation. In this way the works of the poets have become "the songs of nations." [1] This function of the poet, Emerson believes, has been exemplified by great poets in the past. The glory that was Greece, for example, lives not in the works of historians, but in the poems of Homer. Elizabethan England is not truly revealed in the works of historians but in the poetry of Shakespeare; it is as though "Shakspeare had known and reported men, instead of inventing them at his desk" (*Works*, VIII, 44).[2] Furthermore, "Shakspeare immortalizes his characters. They live in every age" (*Journals*, II, 234). The Puritan vision of God's kingdom on earth is not exemplified in what the Puritans did but in Milton's great epic.[3]

The poet in capturing the essence of his nation and his time is not, however, merely serving a national function. Such poetry transcends national boundaries and is, therefore, universal. The poet's material must be cast in the mold of his own age and its traditions, because the poet must maintain an intimate connection with the thought and events of his own time.

> He must bear his share of the common load. He must work with men in houses, and not with their names in books. His needs, appetites, talents, affections, accomplishments, are keys that open to him the beautiful museum of human life (*Works*, I, 177).

The Muse bids Saadi to "Open innumerable doors . . . Those doors are men" (*Works*, IX, 135). Similarly the thunderous tones of the regal Merlin echo the grandeur of nature but also

> With the pulse of manly hearts;
> With the voice of orators;
> With the din of city arts;
> With the cannonade of wars;
> With the marches of the brave;
> And prayers of might from martyrs' cave (*Works*, IX, 120–121).

Shakespeare, Emerson feels, had accomplished this blending of the timely and the timeless:

> The poet needs a ground in popular tradition on which he may

work, and which, again, may restrain his art within the due tem-
perance. It holds him to the people, supplies a foundation for his
edifice, and in furnishing so much work done to his hand, leaves
him at leisure and in full strength for the audacities of his imagination (*Works*, IV, 194).

There is, then, a mutual dependence on the part of the poet and his
people: they furnish the materials out of which his art is created,
and he in turn gives them poems filled with immortal heroes. So it
is with Saadi:

> Most welcome they who need him most,
> They feed the spring which they exhaust;
> For greater need
> Draws better deed: (*Works*, IX, 131).

The second phase of the poet's obligation to society is to reveal
the relationship between man and nature and between man and
nature and God. Emerson found the Plotinian doctrine of emana-
tion helpful in explaining this part of the poet's function. The poet
tells men that God is the center, the source, from which all life and
form emanate. Man partakes of spirit characteristic of beings above
him in the scale at the same time that he partakes of the physical
characteristics of nature and the animal world below him. Janus-
faced, he looks both ways—up to the higher spiritual plane, down
to the lower physical realm. Man occupies the crucial position in
this "Great Chain of Being" and gives symmetry to the whole, for
he unites the poles of existence, the spiritual and the physical.

The pulsation of life and form out from the center, the Source, is
a continuing process. The Heraclitean figure of the flowing river
expresses the idea: life, being, existence—all is like the river which
flows down to the sea; the sea supplies the vapor for clouds which
pour their waters on the land; the waters find their way again to
the river and thence to the sea; and the cycle is repeated. To Emerson, an even more agreeable expression of this concept of flowing
was the Proclean figure of the circle. The perfect figure, the circle
is conceived of as a series of points flowing about a never-changing
center; an arc of the circle, when detached, appears as a straight
line to the senses, but to detach any part from the whole and con-

sider it in and for itself alone gives a distorted view. That is what Emerson refers to when he says in "The Poet":

> For as it is dislocation and detachment from the life of God that makes things ugly, the poet, who re-attaches things to nature and the Whole,—re-attaching even artificial things and violations of nature, to nature, by a deeper insight,—disposes very easily of the most disagreeable facts (*Works*, III, 18–19).

The poet has the obligation of showing men that the seeming "dislocation and detachment" are the result of deception by the senses and hence are not real. Events, actions, facts, thought must be viewed in the light of the Whole in order to understand their proper place and their true significance.

Concerning the relationship of man and nature, Emerson agrees with Wordsworth, who says that the poet "considers man and nature as essentially adapted to each other, and the mind of man as naturally the mirror of the fairest and most interesting properties of nature." [4] It is one of the functions of the poet to show man that his relationship with nature has a dual aspect—the physical and the spiritual.

As Emerson points out in *Nature*, on the physical level nature provides for man a purely utilitarian base for operation, a place in which to live and obtain food and shelter. But since man is naturally able to make better use of the physical environment than animals are able to do, he must be shown that there is a proper use of nature in both its undeveloped and developed state.

Emerson was well aware that the spiritual side of man waits for the development of his physical well being. As he said early in life, "The most enthusiastic philosopher requires to be fed and clothed before he begins his analysis of nature" (*Journals*, I, 261). Although Emerson was naturally more interested in the spiritual than the material, he was not completely antagonistic toward the material concerns of his age. Concurrent with his tendency toward idealism was, in fact, a strongly realistic tendency. His total body of writing shows an active and continuing concern with the material world. This does not mean, however, that he subscribed to the theories of materialistic politicians and businessmen of his time; on the contrary, he was usually their severest critic. But he did not ignore

the utilitarian point of view. Something in his nature allowed him
to rejoice in the masculine strength of the expanding nation and in
the development of the railroad, telegraph, commerce, and industry. He saw that materialism was a characteristic of the time, a
sign of the youth of the nation, and one of the growing pains
through which the nation would pass to something better.

This train of thought in Emerson has important bearing on his
concept of the ways by which the poet shows man the proper use
of the material world. Although the poet, Emerson says, naturally
feels more strongly about things of the spirit, he must not ignore
the prosaic details of everyday life and must attempt to show men
that their own inventions are yet a part of nature. As he explains:

> Readers of poetry see the factory-village and the railway, and
> fancy that the poetry of the landscape is broken up by these; for
> these works of art are not yet consecrated in their reading; but
> the poet sees them fall within the great Order not less than the
> beehive or the spider's geometrical web. Nature adopts them very
> fast into her vital circles, and the gliding train of cars she loves
> like her own (*Works*, III, 19).

The poet reveals that man's inventions are but divinely created
matter taking another form under the creative hand of man. Necessarily, it makes little difference what form the matter takes, so long
as man understands that all things inevitably change. Man's problem is to see through these changes and to understand underlying
principles—the law for man and the law for things. That he can do,
with the guidance of the poet. Emerson's poem "Xenophanes"
shows the unity that stands behind the variety in nature:

> . . . all things
> Are of one pattern made; bird, beast and flower,
> Song, picture, form, space, thought and character
> Deceive us, seeming to be many things,
> And are but one . . . (*Works*, IX, 137).

And in the poem "Woodnotes," the pine tree speaking for nature
says, "Change I may, but I pass not" (*Works*, IX, 57).

Nature, then, is intimately related to man in that it is, on the
lower level, the Great Mother to him, feeding, sustaining, protect-

ing him, but nature has a higher and less evident purpose which the poet reveals to men. On the higher level, nature is the teacher of the profound lessons of the spirit because it reveals perfect natural laws that are the mirror of spiritual laws. Nature exists for man as concrete evidence of God Himself. The poet reveals to man the perfect laws under which nature operates and the organic unity in the whole scheme of nature, which is a reflection of the beauty and perfection of the Creator. Saadi shows how the the poet makes this relationship clear:

> For, whom the Muses smile upon,
> And touch with soft persuasion,
> His words like a storm-wind can bring
> Terror and beauty on their wing;
> In his every syllable
> Lurketh Nature veritable;
> And though he speak in midnight dark,—
> In heaven no star, on earth no spark,—
> Yet before the listener's eye
> Swims the world in ecstasy,
> The forest waves, the morning breaks,
> The pastures sleep, ripple the lakes,
> Leaves twinkle, flowers like persons be,
> And life pulsates in rock or tree,
> Saadi, so far thy words shall reach:
> Suns rise and set in Saadi's speech! (*Works*, IX, 134).

"All men are poets at heart," Emerson says. "They serve nature for bread, but her loveliness overcomes them sometimes" (*Works*, I, 169). The poet takes advantage of man's predilection for nature in his attempt to show the relationship existing between all things throughout the universe. He persuades men to accept his own viewpoint: "The poet casts his eyes on no object, how mean soever, not on a tub or shoe, but it grows poetical in his eye. The whole world is a poem to him" (*Journals*, II, 380).

The poet shows man the pleasure his mind derives from the perception of similitude in dissimilitude. Wordsworth says that this principle is the great spring of activity of the mind.[5] Shelley also speaks of the fusing power of poetry which "marries exultation and horror, grief and pleasure, eternity and change" and subdues to "union under its light yoke all irreconcilable things." [6] It is the function of the poet to harmonize these antagonistic opposites, even as "Merlin's mighty line / Extremes of nature reconciled" (*Works*, IX, 122). In the essay "Character," Emerson describes this reconciliation of opposites:

> Everything in nature is bipolar, or has a positive and a negative pole. There is a male and a female, a spirit and a fact, a north and a south. Spirit is the positive, the event is the negative (*Works*, III, 97).

The poet harmonizes these extremes in the same manner that music brings concord out of discord, as Plato describes it.[7] This polarity is the basis for the second part of Emerson's poem "Merlin":

> Balance-loving Nature
> Made all things in pairs.
> To every foot its antipode;
> Each color with its counter glowed;
> To every tone beat answering tones,
> Higher or graver....
> Hands to hands, and feet to feet,
> In one body grooms and brides;
> Eldest rite, two married sides
> In every mortal meet (*Works*, IX, 123).

Thus it is that the poet makes evident to man the subtle relationship between man, nature, and God. Man and nature are the arcs of the circle which flow naturally and inevitably about its fixed center, which is God; hence a harmony is produced such as Uriel foresaw when he said, "Line in Nature is not found; / Unit and universe are round . . ." (*Works*, IX, 14). Man occupies a central place in this harmonious scheme; he cannot exist without God—but God would not be God without man. Such is the beneficent principle which controls the "each and all," as Emerson had explained earlier in the essay *Nature*.[8]

In his greatest role as Sayer, the poet expresses these concepts for men, and they, recognizing the superior power of expression of the poet, accept the explanation which they themselves cannot put into words. "There is no man," Emerson declares, "who does not anticipate a supersensual utility in the sun and stars, earth and water" (*Works*, III, 5). The poet explains that utility. "Man, never so often deceived still watches for the arrival of the brother who can hold him steady to a truth until he has made it his own" (*Works*, III, 11). The poet is that "brother," as is Saadi "A Brother of the world . . ." (*Works*, IX, 310).

The third and last major function of the poet is that of the "liberating god," a term Emerson borrowed from the Platonists.[9] In this humanitarian role that the poet performs for his fellowmen, the poet frees men from the prison house of their everyday thoughts. Men, Emerson contends, are "On the brink of the waters of life and truth" (*Works*, III, 33), but cannot reach them. They are prone to live timidly in their old thoughts and not reach out for new ones. "The only poetic fact in the life of thousands and thousands," Emerson laments, "is their death. No wonder they specify all the circumstances of the death of another person" (*Journals*, VI, 230). For that reason, there is great need of the poet who "unlocks our chains and admits us to a new scene" (*Works*, III, 33). The poet is aware that "the imagination which intoxicates" him is "not inactive in other men." He knows that

> The use of symbols has a certain power of emancipation and exhilaration for all men. We seem to be touched by a wand which makes us dance, and run about happily, like children. We are like persons who come out of a cave or cellar into the open air. This is the effect on us of tropes, fables, oracles and all poetic forms. Poets are thus liberating gods (*Works*, III, 30).[10]

Emerson's own poetry reveals two aspects of this liberating quality. His Merlin is "the haughty, free and liberating poet" (*Works*, IX, 440) whose utterances are wild and untamed, daring and provocative, tantalizing the mind to be likewise as careless of form and tradition. Merlin is one of "The ancient British bards [who] had for the title of their order, 'Those who are free throughout the world.' They are free, and they make free" (*Works*, III, 32). On the other hand, the gentle Saadi represents the other aspect of the poet as liberator.[11] As "Brother of the world," he is the "joy-giver and enjoyer" who seeks "the living among the dead,— Man in man is imprisonéd . . ." (*Works*, IX, 133). Saadi, "The cheerer of men's hearts," passes unobtrusively through the hall of the lord and the hut of the camel-driver, and his songs filled with the love of man and God are the keys that open all doors.

In his role as "liberating god," the poet enriches men's lives by revealing glimpses of the eternal world beyond sensory experience. Of this land of the spirit, "he knows and tells; he is the only teller of news, for he was present and privy to the appearance which he describes" (*Works*, III, 8). But he must translate his vision into language that men understand. "The poet has a new thought; he has a whole new experience to unfold; he will tell us how it was with him, and all men will be the richer in his fortune" (*Works*, III, 10).

On the lower plane of everyday living, the poet as "liberating god" is the "joy-giver" who shows men that if they go about their tasks with unselfishness and with dignity, a feeling of joy and well-being will be the reward. A sustaining joy of being alive and of being part of such a perfect universe may be theirs upon recognition that they are a necessary part of the divine creation. Nature, too, reflects this joy in the physical beauty it displays for man's pleasure. All men have the impulse to seek out and enjoy beauty if they will not allow this impulse to be overwhelmed in the affairs of the everyday world. "We are greatly more poetic than we know," Emerson maintains; "poets in our drudgery, poets in our eyes, and ears, and skin" (*Journals*, VI, 191). It is the poet who keeps men aware of this quality of imagination. As Emerson says, "the poet says nothing but what helps somebody; let others be distracted with cares, he is exempt. All their pleasures are tinged with pain. All his pains are edged with pleasure. The gladness he imparts he shares" (*Works*, VIII, 37).

In summary, the three-fold function of the poet in society involves the preservation of the fame of heroes and sages in the immortal songs of nations, interpretation of spiritual and physical laws governing man's place in the universe, and the liberation of men's minds. These duties are among the most important in any society and make the poet an integral part of the community as a man speaking to men. The benefits are mutual. As Emerson says, "If we

believed no poet survived on the planet, nature would be tedious"
(*Journals*, III, 449). Until that time when every man would be his
own poet—a possibility which Emerson could imagine—there would
continue to be a vital need for the poet in society, and each age
would need its own poet to give it expression.

CHAPTER THREE

The Poet's Use of Subject Matter and Form

THE "MEANS AND MATERIALS" by which the poet makes his message known is the third topic in Emerson's essay "The Poet." It is soon evident that Emerson does not intend to discuss the technical aspects of poetry. Temperamentally opposed to systems, Emerson characteristically says elsewhere, "No practical rules for the poem, no working-plan was ever drawn up" (*Works*, XII, 72), and he warns, "Don't rattle your rules in our ears" (*Works*, XII, 305).[1] Despite his reluctance to formulate a system, his comments on subject matter and form in "The Poet" and elsewhere in his *Journals* and letters reveal an implicit faith in the organic principle.

"Thought makes everything fit for use" (*Works*, III, 17), Emerson asserts. Thus the poet has at his command the entire range of man and nature, as indicated in the essay *Nature*:

> By a few strokes he [the poet] delineates, as on air, the sun, the mountain, the camp, the city, the hero, the maiden, not different from what we know them, but only lifted from the ground and afloat before the eye. He unfixes the land and the sea, makes them revolve around the axis of his primary thought, and disposes them anew (*Works*, I, 51–52).

The universal appeal of nature provides a vehicle for the poet to reach a wide audience. In "The Poet," Emerson asks:

Who loves nature? Who does not? Is it only poets, and men of leisure and cultivation, who live with her? No; but also hunters, farmers, grooms and butchers, though they express their affections in their choice of life and not in their choice of words. The writer wonders what the coachman or the hunter values in riding, in horses and dogs. It is not superficial qualities. When you talk with him he holds these at as slight a rate as you. His worship is sympathetic; he has no definitions, but he is commanded in nature by the living power which he feels to be there present (*Works*, III, 15).

The poet as Sayer supplies the "definitions" lacking in the vocabulary of the ordinary man and describes the "living power" that resides in nature. The poet, using the "ladder of beauty" Emerson describes in *Nature*, leads men in the ascent from delight in the surface beauty of nature, to intellectual contemplation, to nature's spiritual meaning. The poet's capability of using nature in this way comes only after he has served his apprenticeship in contemplation of nature and cultivation of intuition in solitude. Emerson's autobiographical poem "The Poet" dramatizes the struggle for such transcendent expression:

> Eager for good, not hating ill,
> Thanked Nature for each stroke she dealt;
> On his tense chords all strokes were felt,
> The good, the bad with equal zeal,
> He asked, he only asked, to feel (*Works*, IX, 316).

Patience is necessary for the poet to learn "how it is with him" before he can, as a representative man, tell men how it is with them. Emerson's Saadi knew the discipline of waiting until the inspiration was strong enough:

> Saadi held the Muse in awe,
> She was his mistress and his law;
> A twelvemonth he could silence hold,
> Nor ran to speak till she him told;
> He felt the flame, the fanning wings,
> Nor offered words till they were things. . . (*Works*, IX, 325).

Shakespeare had this transcendent quality of poetry—sometimes

Emerson calls it "the grand design" or the power that "cleanses and mans me." Emerson asserts, "Shakespeare possesses the power of subordinating nature for the purpose of expression, beyond all poets. His imperial muse tosses the creation like a bauble from hand to hand, and uses it to embody any caprice of thought that is uppermost in his mind" (*Works*, I, 52).

But Shakespeare was also capable of working "the miracle of mythologizing every fact of common life" (*Works*, IX, 502), and Emerson would not have the poet forget the dualism of man who lives in a world of things seen and unseen. Emerson did not forget; as he says in "The Method of Nature":

> I do not wish in attempting to paint a man, to describe an air-fed, unimpassioned, impossible ghost. My eyes and ears are revolted by any neglect of the physical facts, the limitations of man. And yet one who conceives the true order of nature, and beholds the visible as proceeding from the invisible, cannot state his thought without seeming to those who study the physical laws to do them some injustice. There is an intrinsic defect in the organ. Language overstates. Statements of the infinite are usually felt to be unjust to the finite, and blasphemous (*Works*, I, 198).

The dualism of man is further reflected in what he does; there are men of action and men of reflection. One function of the poet, it will be remembered, is to create the songs of nations in which both types appear—the heroes and the sages. The poet uses the noble and virtuous acts of heroes—often complemented, Emerson says, by the beauty of nature in which they are performed—to reveal to all men their own potential for such deeds. As Emerson declares in *Representative Men*:

> As to what we call the masses, the common men,—there are no common men. All men are at last of a size; and true art is only possible on the conviction that every talent has its apotheosis somewhere (*Works*, IV, 31).

Since "Thought makes everything fit for use," the poet has the whole range of human experience, from the heroic down to the menial, to shadow forth his message. Saadi, who was equally at home with lords in halls and poor men in huts, learned the important lesson of humility from Hassan, the camel-driver.[2]

For his subject matter, then, the poet has the whole of the
created universe to achieve his end of showing man the important
place he occupies in the divine scheme. His poems must show
that "Man carries the world in his head" (*Works*, III, 183) and
convince him that "God hid the whole world in thy heart"
(*Works*, IX, 56).

It was long assumed that Emerson had an imperfect sense of
form in poetry, because his poetic practices were at variance with
those accepted as the best in his day. More recent critics have
defended his poetry and his concept of organic form.[3] Although
he did not systemize his ideas of form in poetry, statements scattered through his works reveal a consistent pattern.

Emerson sometimes speaks of the "design" or "the grand design" in poetry, by which he seems to mean the scope of ideas
behind the poem rather than any conventional form. In "The
Poet" he refers to books in which he finds beautiful parts or
"gems," but then he laments in one of his own poems, "Ah, but I
miss the grand design" (*Works*, IX, 331). Thus, it appears that
he always looked for an ulterior plan in poetry, a design that
transcends the form of the poem on the printed page. He does
not discount the importance of recognizable form, for it is the
link between the poet's mind and the minds of men. He says in
"The Poet," "The argument is secondary, the finish of the verse
is primary" (*Works*, III, 9). By "argument" Emerson apparently
means the concept or the dramatic continuity in the poem, and
by "finish" he means the welding of thought and form, not versification. "For it is not metres," he continues, "but a metre-making
argument that makes a poem." That is, the idea in the poem must
be so completely fused with the way the idea is expressed that
the two appear to be one. In addition, he maintains that a poem is
"a thought so passionate and alive that like the spirit of a plant or
animal it has an architecture of its own, and adorns nature with a
new thing" (*Works*, III, 9–10). The poem, then, has its own individual unity; it has organic form.

Emerson found the concept of organic unity expressed in
Plato,[4] but Coleridge's explanation made it more graphic:

No work of true genius dares want its appropriate form, neither indeed is there any danger of this. As it must not, so genius can not be lawless; for it is ever this that constitutes its genius—the power of acting creatively under laws of its own origination. . . . The form is mechanic, when on any given material we impress a predetermined form, not necessarily arising out of the properties of the material—as when to a mass of wet clay we give whatever shape we wish it to retain when hardened. The organic form, on the other hand, is innate; it shapes, as it develops itself from within, and the fullness of its development is one and the same with the perfection of its outward form. Such as the life is, such is the form. Nature, the prime genial artist, inexhaustible in diverse power, is equally inexhaustible in forms. . . .[5]

Emerson had, of course, accepted the organic theory long before he wrote the essay "The Poet." [6] His interest in botany and biology, enhanced by his visit to the Garden of Plants in Paris in 1833, impressed the theory more firmly on his mind.

According to Emerson, use of organic form is congenial to the poet who, by his nature, understands the principle involved. Since unity is the primary characteristic of the universe, the poet constructs his poems in such a way that they reflect that unity. He knows, for instance, that the whole universe is at his disposal, and he constantly searches for natural forms, heroic action, and objects large and small that can be transformed into poetic material. He knows that "He who makes a good sentence or a good verse exercises a power very strictly analogous to his [power] who makes a fine statue . . . " (*Journals*, III, 395). He knows also that the organic process in nature is his best model; "Nature mixes fact and thought to evoke a poem" (*Journals*, V, 287). Also, the poet fuses nature and man to achieve an organic whole; for "Natural history by itself has no value; it is like a single sex; but marry it to human history, and it is poetry" (*Journals*, III, 326–327). "A poem is made up of thoughts," Emerson asserts, "each of which filled the whole sky of the poet in its turn" (*Journals*, III, 335). But these thoughts, appealing as they may be separately, must ultimately be made subservient to an eternal truth, which may be expressed only by the welding of thought and form into an organic whole that belies the process by which it was done. As Emerson expresses it:

> In Poetry we say we require the miracle. The bee flies among the
> flowers, and gets mint and marjoram, and generates a new prod-
> uct, which is not mint and marjoram, but honey; the chemist
> mixes hydrogen and oxygen to yield a new product, which is
> not these, but water; and the poet listens to conversation and be-
> holds all objects in Nature, to give back, not them, but a new and
> transcendent whole (*Works*, VIII, 16–17).[7]

In "The Poet" Emerson compares the poems of the poet to the
statue of a sculptor who, when inspired by a beautiful dawn,
creates a beautiful youth before whom all visitors become silent.
Likewise, the poet in giving expression to his thought creates
something new out of the materials that are old, and his readers
see familiar objects in a new light. "The expression is organic,"
Emerson declares, "or the new type which things themselves take
when liberated" (*Works*, III, 24). Emerson compares this metamorphosis of thought into form to the effect of physical forms on
the senses; "as the form of the thing is reflected by the eye, so the
soul of the thing is reflected by melody" (*Works*, III, 25).

Some poets of the past, Emerson believes, have instinctively
produced this organic form. Milton, for example, is able "to draw
after Nature a life of man" (*Works*, XII, 254), and Emerson suggests that perhaps "a universal poetry began and ended" with
Shakespeare (*Parnassus*, Preface, v). Homer, Dante, Chaucer, and
Shakespeare had seen "the splendor of meaning that plays over the
visible world" (*Works*, IV, 216), and they reflect this profound
meaning in their immortal poems. In his poem "Bacchus," Emerson seeks inspiration which he calls

> Wine of wine,
> Blood of the world,
> Form of forms, and mould of statures,
> That I intoxicated,
> And by the draught assimilated,
> May float at pleasure through all natures . . .
> (*Works*, IX, 125).

Such insight enables the poet to look "to the cause and life: it
proceeds from within outward . . . and draws its means and the
style of its architecture from within . . ." (*Works*, I, 218).

On the level of composition, the poet employs the tools of his craft in putting his poems in objective form—words, symbols, proverbs, and story.[8] In the ascending order of units of composition, Emerson places great importance on the word. He says, "In reading prose, I am sensible as soon as a sentence drags, but in reading poetry, as soon as one word drags" (*Journals*, IX, 214). As has been discussed in connection with the poet as "Namer" and "Language-maker," Emerson believes that words were in the beginning the special creation of poets. "The poets made all the words," he asserts, "and therefore language is the archives of history" (*Works*, III, 21). And he adds, "Every word was once a poem." In *Nature* he argues that "Words are signs of natural facts" (*Works*, I, 25), and since natural facts are symbols of spiritual facts, words have both a concrete existence as things and a spiritual significance as well.[9] Words, then, as the smallest element in form, have a special significance. "There is no choice of words for him who clearly sees the truth," Emerson asserts. "That provides him with the best word" (*Works*, VIII, 33). Furthermore, "The manner of using language is surely the most decisive test of intellectual power" (*Journals*, II, 449).

The poet, always aware that he writes for men and not for poets alone, seeks those words that will not only capture the form and meaning of the material which he uses but which will have instant appeal. He is aware, for example, that "The language of the street is always strong," and he will find, as Emerson did, "the stinging rhetoric of a rattling oath" an example of the vitality of words. "Cut these words and they would bleed," Emerson asserts; "they are vascular and alive; they walk and run" (*Journals*, V, 420).[10] It may be necessary for the poet to use "low" words in order to reinforce his meaning. Emerson justifies such usage when he says in "The Poet":

> The vocabulary of an omniscient man would embrace words and images excluded from polite conversation. What would be base, or even obscene, to the obscene, becomes illustrious, spoken in a new connection of thought (*Works*, III, 17).[11]

On a higher level, when the poet puts the world "under the mind for verb and noun" (*Works*, III, 20), he is forced to choose words with even more suggestive power. Such words must carry meaning on the literal, figurative, and emblematic levels. They must serve as conductors to transfer the reader from an initial impression of form, through a moment of pleasurable recognition of the figurative sense, to the ultimate spiritual fact that the word represents. This reaction must be spontaneous. Words so successfully used immediately transmit the poet's meaning; "for in every word he speaks he rides on them as the horses of thought" (*Works*, III, 21).[12]

The symbol is the second element of organic expression and is the outgrowth of the use of the right word. "I had rather have a good symbol of my thought, or a good analogy," Emerson announces, "than the suffrage of Kant or Plato" (*Works*, VIII, 13).[13] Symbolic language is possible because words originally used for natural facts came to be used for states of mind and spiritual facts. "Things admit of being used as symbols," Emerson affirms, "because nature is a symbol, in the whole, and in every part" (*Works*, III, 13). Consequently, "The poet discovers that what men value as substances have a higher value as symbols; that Nature is the immense shadow of a man" (*Works*, VIII, 23). The use of symbolic language has the power of exhilaration and emancipation that gives to the mind an exquisite pleasure and thereby makes the truth revealed more memorable. In "The Poet" Emerson shows how poets become "liberating gods" by their superior use of symbolic language. But the use of symbols is not confined to poets; all classes of people use them, Emerson maintains. Poets and philosophers are no more intrigued with their symbols than are other people with their party symbols, national emblems, heraldic devices, and flags. "The people fancy they hate poetry," he concludes, "and they are all poets and mystics!" (*Works*, III, 16–17). Thus, symbolic language is universal, but only the poet, who is by nature the language-maker, is able to create new symbols so vital and alive that they pass into the common language. For this reason, the poet is valued above the mystic who, though also an inventor of symbols, "nails a symbol to one sense," as Emerson feels that Swedenborg did.[14] In other words, the poet recognizes that "All symbols are fluxional" and cease to be vital when too long used for the same meaning. The poet "sees through the flowing vest the firm nature, and can declare it" by the use of symbols (*Works*, III, 37).

Regarded from the structural standpoint, the symbol has a multiple aspect. On the lower level it appeals to the mind because it exhibits basic thought in a new cloak; on the higher level it tends to lose its identity in the spiritual fact it represents. It flows, as it were, from the first form into the second in the manner suggested by the Plotinian theory of the flowing of all things in which all forms are ever tending to flow into other forms. The word itself is one form; in its symbolic sense it is another; and in its ultimate meaning it is a third. As a consequence of this fluxional nature of the symbol, the mind in making the transference from the word to the final meaning experiences the sensation of seeing one form glide into another and yet another. Emerson captures the idea of flowing forms in his poem "Woodnotes":

> Onward and on, the eternal Pan,
> Who layeth the world's incessant plan,
> Halteth never in one shape,
> But forever doth escape,
> Like wave or flame, into new forms
> Of gem, and air, of plants, and worms (*Works*, IX, 58).

The profound meanings that may be expressed by symbols do not compel the poet to search for special materials; "Small and mean things serve as well as great symbols," Emerson declares. In fact, "The meaner the type by which a law is expressed, the more pungent it is, and the more lasting in the memories of men" (*Works*, III, 17). The poet's power to convert the fact "from a particular into a general proposition" (*Journals*, VIII, 571) gives efficiency to the symbol, and this is the power that puts "eyes and a tongue into every dumb and inanimate object" (*Works*, III, 20). Concerning this power, Emerson says in "Art and Criticism":

> The power of the poet is in controlling these symbols; in using every fact in Nature, however great and stable, as a fluent symbol, and in measuring his strength by the facility with which he makes the mood of mind give its color to things. The world, history, the

powers of Nature,—he can make them speak what sense he will
(*Works*, XII, 300).

This power over symbols arises from the dual activity of the
poet's mind. The capacity to see through appearances surrounding
natural objects is accompanied by a creative power which invests
those objects with meaning. Or, it might be said that the actual *seeing* is not only a penetration into the essence of the object, but an
interpretation of its ultimate meaning as well—a power that only a
highly intuitive mind possesses. This subtle interchange of perception and creation is explained in a passage in the *Journals*:

> [The] Poet sees the stars, because he makes them. Perception
> makes. We can only see what we make, all our desires are pro-
> creant. Perception has a destiny. I notice that all poetry comes, or
> all becomes poetry, when we look from within and are using all
> as if the mind made it (*Journals*, VIII, 321).[15]

The concept is stated also in the poem "The Poet":

> And yet, dear stars, I know ye shine
> Only by needs and loves of mine;
> Light-loving, light-asking life in me
> Feeds those eternal lamps I see (*Works*, IX, 317).

The next larger unit of composition in the poem to which Emerson attaches great importance is the line. This unit may be a phrase,
a clause, or a complete sentence, in which so much thought is con-
centrated that it is a living thing, that is, *sententia*. Evidently such is
Emerson's meaning when he says, "Every poem must be made up
of lines that are poems" (*Journals*, VII, 523).[16] These lines become
part of the proverbial speech, such as Emerson himself was good at
creating.[17] These memorable lines are probably what Emerson refers to as "lustres." They are intimately associated with proverbs,
epigrams, and apothegms which he treasured. In *Nature* he says,
"the proverbs of nations consist usually of a natural fact," and he
cites many very common ones as proof. "In their primary sense,"
he continues, "these are trivial facts, but we repeat them for the
value of their analogical import" (*Works*, I, 33).[18] These small
units of expression act as a mutual meeting ground for the poet and

his audience; they attract the reader by their terse cogency and spur him on to seek the total meaning of the poem.[19] The poet continually creates new ones and uses old ones in fresh connections in the same manner that he does symbols.

The fourth element of composition in the poem is the "fable," by which Emerson means the story, or the narration, or the continuity of impression of the poem. This larger unit is naturally a fusion of words, symbols, and lines into the vehicle for carrying the ultimate meaning. Consequently, he says, "the fable or myth must hold, or it is worth no man's while to read it" (*Journals*, VII, 114). Significantly, Emerson uses the words "fable or myth" for he believes that great truths can most effectively be shown in these forms. He found Plato's myths appealing and refers to some of them many times. These myths, he believes, not only give pleasure in themselves, but symbolize eternal truths. As he says, "I like that poetry which, without aiming to be allegorical, is so. Which, sticking close to its subject, and that perhaps trivial, can yet be applied to the life of man and government of God and be found to hold" (*Journals*, III, 544).[20] Since "The beauty of the fable proves the importance of the sense," (*Works*, III, 15) it must be a "good story, and its meaning must hold as pure truth" (*Parnassus*, Preface, viii). The story, then, is the final synthesis, the effecting of which Emerson remarks upon in "Poetry and Imagination":

> . . . there is a third step which poetry takes, and which seems higher than the others, namely, creation, or ideas taking forms of their own,—when the poet invents the fable, and invents the language which his heroes speak (*Works*, VIII, 38–39).

If the exact words and symbols are chosen, the ideas they represent fuse themselves into an organic whole; the objective form is latent in the ideas themselves and the final form becomes inevitable.

As for rhyme and rhythm as part of poetic form, it is difficult to determine Emerson's attitude, because he frequently speaks of them as one and the same, or as "melody," as in the essay "Poetry and Imagination." In that essay in a section entitled "Melody, Rhyme, Form," he discusses in general terms the attraction rhyme and rhythm have for people, especially for children and young people.

This appeal, he says, may be likened to the universal attraction of music. "Rhyme," he contends, "is a pretty good measure of the latitude and opulence of a writer" (*Works*, VIII, 49); then, he cites Spenser, Marlowe, and Chapman as masters of rhyme and rhythm. Since there will always be those people who like these elements most in poetry,

> Let Poetry then pass, if it will, into music and rhyme. That is the form which itself puts on. We do not enclose watches in wooden, but in crystal cases, and rhyme is the transparent frame that allows almost the pure architecture of thought to become visible to the mental eye. Substance is much, but so are mode and form much (*Works*, VIII, 52–53).

This musical power of poetry, Emerson suggests, has enabled some "masters" to "rise above themselves to strains which charm their readers, and which neither any competitor could outdo, nor the bard himself again equal." Evidence of these "strains," Emerson says, are to be found in Keats, Jonson, Waller, Herbert, Lovelace, and Collins (*Works*, VIII, 54–55).

These views on rhyme and rhythm are expressed in the general manner befitting a popular lecture, as "Poetry and Imagination" was, but there is indication in a few places of the earlier attitude toward rhyme in "The Poet." He says, for example, that the mature mind demands more subtle rhymes and that the "real rhymes" are "the correspondence of parts in Nature,—acid and alkali, body and mind, man and maid, character and history, action and reaction . . . " (*Works*, VIII, 48–49). In this same vein the second half of Emerson's poem "Merlin" uses the word "rhyme" as an extended metaphor to show that "Balance-loving Nature / Made all things in pairs," the implication being that the intellect enjoys these echoes of correspondences as much as the ear is pleased with the music of repeated sounds in poetry.

Rhyme and rhythm are organic and cannot be separated from the idea in poetry, as indeed they are in "stock poetry," that is, verse in which sound and metrical virtuosity obscure the idea. Thought must dominate form. Further evidence of Emerson's preference for ideas is the section on "prose poets" in the essay "Poetry and Imagination." Those he lists are Thomas Taylor,[21] Burke, Thomas

Browne, and St. Augustine. Emerson shared with many of the English Romantics the belief that prose can also be "poetry." [22]

In summary, the completed poem is the objective form of the poet's subjective impressions. In the poem that has perfect organic form, subject and object have become one: every word is the right word, every image is new and alive with transcendent meaning, some lines are so memorable that they are immortal, rhyme and rhythm are dictated by ideas, and the whole poem exhibits in its outward form the inner unity that shaped it. The poem is the sum of all of its parts as well as something more. Like the living organism that it resembles in unity, the poem is a complete fusion of natural fact, thought, inevitable form, and spiritual fact. Such a poem is like the plant that evolves from the seed, through root, stem, branch, leaf, flower, fruit, and back to seed; each part grows naturally out of the preceding part and the whole exemplifies the potential of the seed from which that plant and no other could have sprung. The poem, moreover, is the organic expression of the mind of the poet who has scanned the whole range of man and the universe, and who has translated his vision into a form as beautiful and true as nature itself.

CHAPTER FOUR

The Ideal Poet

IN HIS PURSUIT of a definition of the nature, function, and art of the poet, Emerson's thinking in its involuted and convoluted movement resembles his favorite figure, the circle which, conceived of as a series of points revolving around a center, always ascends and thus becomes the spiral. On the one hand, he insists that the poet must be solidly based in "the dark wet soil" of reality, but he must also be the "liberating god" whose inspired utterances strike off the chains of tradition and convention that bind men's minds and the seer whose prophetic vision carries them along the curves of the ascending spiral to the very heights of human imagination where "the air is music." But beyond, always above the reach of such a superior mortal, stands the pristine ideal—the stark, supreme *idea*—poet. Along the ever-ascending arcs of that spiral stand human incarnations of the idea, variously referred to as "true" poets and "the potential or ideal man." In "Poetry and Imagination," Emerson says:

> . . . when we describe man as poet, and credit him with the triumphs of the art, we speak of the potential or ideal man,—not found now in any one person. You must go through a city or a nation, and find one faculty here, one there, to build the true poet withal. Yet all men know the portrait when it is drawn, and it is part of religion to believe its possible incarnation (*Works*, VIII, 26).

The fact that, in Emerson's opinion, all men do recognize the image of the ideal poet attests to the universality of the idea and therefore validates judging poets by such a high standard. On the other hand, Emerson would have his ideal poet no mere abstraction; his insistence upon the dual nature of man and art prevents his setting up an abstraction as an ideal. Man cannot completely transcend his nature, which is a balance between matter and spirit, else he becomes pure spirit and is no longer man. Rather, the ideal is the perfect balance of matter and spirit and of the uses of Reason and Understanding. The ideal poet, then, is man as poet maintaining this perfect balance.

As has been seen, the poet differs from ordinary men in degree, not in kind. Similarly, the poet differs from the ideal poet in the same manner. It is the heightening of the characteristics of man as poet which produces the ideal poet, who is superior to the poet in the same way that the poet is superior to ordinary men, that is, by a fuller development of the innate powers common to all men. The ideal poet represents the full development of the potential in man as poet. If the qualities which distinguish the poet are developed to their maximum potential, he has the power to transcend the limitations within which most poets must be content to function. Transcendency, as described in the essay "Poetry and Imagination," is that power which enables the ideal poet to see steadily and whole the truth which even the greatest poets of history have seen only partially and by glimpses; the ideal poet is able to transmit the truth that he sees to less gifted men so that it enriches their daily lives. In other words, the ideal poet is not, like the pure mystic, translated by his vision out of this world. He has the power to live in both worlds of man's dual experience and to master both. For this reason, the ideal poet serves a basic need in society which the mystic cannot fulfill, since the mystic is not able to express his experiences coherently or to share his exaltation with other men.

The characteristics and functions of the ideal poet may be summarized as follows:

> He is a man speaking to men. (The special meaning Emerson attaches to "man" in this context involves powers of the soul developed to their highest possible level. Man in his pristine state

was fully in command of these powers; he "fell" from this ideal state when he came to depend upon Understanding more than Reason and became a "dwarf of himself." The ideal poet is man returned to this original state in which the perfect balance between matter and spirit and Reason and Understanding is restored; he has reclaimed his rightful heritage as a man.)

He has developed more completely than other men his innate powers as a divine being.

He depends on Reason to ascertain truth, although he does not ignore Understanding.

He incorporates all phases of native genius.

He is the seer whose perceptions not only penetrate to final meanings but comprehend immediately their full import.

He is the prophet whose knowledge of universal law permits the foreseeing of events and actions in the light of that law.

He is the Sayer whose ability to express truth in words of divine fire exceeds all others.

He is a truly representative man.

He is Man Thinking, in whom there is a perfect balance of the attributes of action, reflection, and expression. He is completely the mirror of his age at the same time that he transcends his age and is representative of man in all ages.

He is the man of Beauty.

He understands the true nature of Beauty, in which inhere the qualities of Truth and Goodness.

He sees beauty in all things.

He creates beauty in the form of poetry for the enjoyment of all men.

He is the supreme artist.

The profound ideas to which he gives form share in the permanency of the eternal truths they represent. The form of his poetry is dictated by the ideas it expresses.

The tools of expression he employs are used with such felicity that they give full power to his thought.

He possesses powers of transcendency.

He transcends human limitations more frequently than other men.

He enables other men to transcend limitations through his art.

Emerson sometimes used the great poets of history (Homer, Dante, Chaucer, Shakespeare, and Milton) to illustrate various phases of the attributes and functions of the ideal poet and his art. These great poets are usually referred to as "eternal men" because of the universality of their achievements, as compared to lesser poets whom Emerson calls "contemporary men." But when Emerson thinks in terms of the ideal poet, he indicates that even these great poets fall short in some respects; as he said in the essay "The Poet," ". . . when we adhere to the ideal of the poet, we have our difficulties even with Milton and Homer" (*Works*, III, 38). The practical value of Emerson's concept of the ideal poet may be indicated by measuring some of the great poets of history against it. Shakespeare and Milton are the best examples because Emerson's commentary on them is much more extensive than on Homer, Dante, and Chaucer.

Emerson's high regard for Shakespeare is evident in the choice of him to represent man as poet in the volume *Representative Men*. Emerson's attitude toward Shakespeare tends toward romantic idolatry, as Robert P. Falk has pointed out,[1] although others have accused Emerson of lack of appreciation of that poet. From the Shakespeare Society papers, which he borrowed from Longfellow, and from his reading in the drama and history of the Elizabethan period, Emerson obtained information for the limited historical perspective evident in his essay on Shakespeare in *Representative Men*. He was not, of course, sufficiently familiar with Renaissance drama to see the extent to which Shakespeare actually followed tradition and convention,[2] as twentieth-century scholarship has revealed. Though Emerson tended to agree with the Romantic commentators that Shakespeare's astounding genius was exceptional and not to be explained, he did state that Shakespeare was a most indebted man, by which he means that Shakespeare took whatever was at hand and followed established forms. Even so, Emerson preferred to think of Shakespeare as the untutored genius warbling his woodnotes wild; such an interpretation fits perfectly Emerson's doctrine of natural genius, which is so important in his concept of the ideal poet.

Shakespeare, when compared to the ideal of the nature of the poet, has certain faults. Emerson does not indicate that he considered Shakespeare to be a man (in Emerson's full sense of that word) as the ideal poet is. Although Shakespeare undoubtedly has great powers as an individual, he does not reveal the same degree of dependence upon Reason that the ideal poet does. On the other hand, Shakespeare approximates the ideal in native genius. Emerson is usually so dazzled by the evidence he sees of genius in Shakespeare that he can seldom be critical. No poet exceeds or even equals this "first of men." He is "undeniably an original and unapproached bard," (*Journals*, III, 329) who proves that "not by books are great poets made" (*Journals*, V, 126).

In measuring Shakespeare against the ideal of the function of the poet, certain shortcomings are apparent. Although he meets two of the requirements for the poet as Man Thinking—reflection and perception—he does not explicitly exemplify the man of action. In Emerson's time, positive knowledge of Shakespeare's actions as a man and citizen was so limited that little could be said about his actions; this fact enhanced the mystery of his inexplicable genius. Emerson does speculate in an early journal entry that Shakespeare probably "deplored his own way of living . . ." (*Journals*, III, 290). There is criticism by implication of his lack of leadership in the statement that Shakespeare did not strike out into new fields of expression but rather accepted the drama as his medium and was content to entertain man as "master of the revels." [3] On the other hand, Shakespeare's work is representative to the ideal degree. The history of Elizabethan England and the histories of numerous types of men are to be found in his plays. Moreover, his work is not only completely representative of his time, but also contains those universal elements that enable it to live for all times. The greatness of Shakespeare's work was not, in fact, fully understood in his time; it was not appreciated fully, Emerson contends, until the nineteenth century.

Certainly, Shakespeare fulfills the requirement of the ideal poet as the man of Beauty. Paragraph after paragraph of the essay on Shakespeare in *Representative Men* pays glowing tribute to the beauty that Shakespeare creates. This beauty carries with it the joy and pleasure so beloved by men:

> One more royal trait properly belongs to the poet. I mean his cheerfulness, without which no man can be a poet,—for beauty is his aim. He loves virtue, not for its obligation but for its grace: he delights in the world, in man, in woman, for the lovely light that sparkles from them. Beauty, the spirit of joy and hilarity, he sheds over the universe. . . . His name suggests joy and emancipation to the heart of men. . . . He touches nothing that does not

borrow health and longevity from his festal style (*Works*, IV, 215–216).

Shakespeare's ability to create this joyous beauty caused Emerson to place him above Milton and all other poets as the man of Beauty.

In artistry Shakespeare meets the test of the ideal. His creative genius remains unmatched in the world. Emerson marvels that "he could create not one or two, but so manifold classes and individuals, and each perfect" (*Journals*, III, 451). In his poetry, "the thought constructs the tune" (*Works*, IV, 195). He is absolute master of all of the means of expression known to poets and can use them as he will.

The ideal poet's power of transcendency is possessed to a great degree by Shakespeare. Through his art, men have since his time been able to experience vicariously the exaltations he felt in his moments of inspiration. Although he shows greater evidence of this power than any poet who has ever lived, he falls short of the ideal. In the essay on Shakespeare in *Representative Men*, after exploring every possible means of praising the poet, Emerson devotes about three pages to a final assessment of his values, shutting his ears, he says, "to the reverberations of his fame" (*Works*, IV, 216). Although Shakespeare employed the whole of nature and the visible world as symbols of his thought, he did not go beyond the apparent beauty of the symbols to their ultimate meanings:

> He rested in their beauty; and never took the step which seemed inevitable to such genius, namely to explore the virtue which resides in these symbols and imparts this power:—what is that which they themselves say? He converted the elements which waited on his command, into entertainments. He was master of the revels to mankind (*Works*, IV, 217).

In another connection, Emerson says, "Shakspear's poetry must suffer that deduction that it is an exhibition and amusement, and is not expected to be eaten and drunk as the bread of life by the people" (*Journals*, VIII, 353). In addition, in comparing Milton to Shakespeare, Emerson declares, "The creations of Shakespeare are cast into the world of thought to no further end than to delight. Their intrinsic beauty is their cause for being" (*Works*, XII, 277).

Emerson's criticism centers in Shakespeare's use of the drama as his chief medium of expression; he laments, for instance, that the sonnets are overshadowed by interest in the plays. Shakespeare, Emerson feels, was content to be master of the revels rather than the great teacher and leader which his genius implies; he was content to amuse rather than to balance amusement with profound and more explicit teaching; he was content to create beauty without making explicit its relationship with truth and goodness. There is no consistent "moral tone" or "moral sentiment" in Shakespeare such as is evident in Milton. Shakespeare exploits the appearances in the beautiful world which he creates but does not explore the eternal meanings, the essences, which stand back of his beautiful creation. And yet, supreme genius that he is in imagination and creative ability, Shakespeare, more nearly than any man who has ever lived, approximates the ideal poet; consequently, Emerson chose him to represent man as poet in *Representative Men*.

Not without some misgivings did Emerson give that place to Shakespeare rather than to Milton, whose *Paradise Lost*, Emerson said, inevitably lay alongside the Bible on living room tables. Oliver Wendell Holmes was perhaps the first to point out the spiritual kinship between Emerson and Milton. In Milton, Emerson sees and approves the high ethical character which motivated his art and which is the foundation of all great art. Milton's profound concern with the ultimate values in life produces the element of "morale" or "moral sentiment" which Emerson finds so appealing. Milton's own desire for personal moral perfection finds a sympathetic response in Emerson:

> Milton describes himself . . . as enamoured of moral perfection. He did not love it more than I. That which I cannot yet declare has been my angel from childhood until now. It has separated me from men. It has watered my pillow, it has driven sleep from my bed. It has tortured me for my guilt. It has inspired me with hope. It cannot be defeated by my defeats. It cannot be questioned, though all the martyrs apostatize. It is always the glory that shall be revealed; it is the 'open secret' of the universe; and it is only the feebleness and dust of the observer that makes it future, and the whole *is* now potentially in the bottom of his heart. It is the soul of religion. Keeping my eye on this, I understand all heroism, the history of loyalty and of martyrdom and of bigotry, the heat

of the Methodists, the nonconformity of the Dissenter, the patience of the Quaker (*Journals*, III, 208–209).

Emerson also agrees with Milton's belief in inspiration and the
triple nature of poetry—that of truth, goodness, and beauty.[4] Furthermore, Emerson respects and admires Milton's reverent attitude
toward the divine commission as poet and prophet; Emerson says
of him, "while young, his spirit is already communing with itself
and stretching out in its colossal proportions and yearning for the
destiny he was appointed to fulfil" (*Journals*, I, 71).

For these reasons, Milton exemplifies many aspects of the ideal
poet, but not all of them.

Milton, when compared to the ideal of the nature of the poet,
comes nearer to meeting the test as a *man* than Shakespeare does.
Milton's power to inspire other men to virtue, Emerson contends,
is greater than that of any man in literary history; "Virtue goes
out of him into others," Emerson says:

> As a poet, Shakespeare undoubtedly transcends, and far surpasses
> him in his popularity with foreign nations; but Shakespeare is a
> voice merely; who and what he was that sang, that sings, we know
> not. Milton stands erect, commanding, still visible as a man among
> men, and reads the laws of the moral sentiment to the new-born
> race. . . . no man, in these later ages, and few men ever, possessed
> so great a conception of the manly character. Better than any
> other he has discharged the office of every great man, namely, to
> raise the idea of Man in the minds of his contemporaries and of
> posterity,—to draw after Nature a life of man, exhibiting such a
> composition of grace, of strength and of virtue, as poet had not
> described nor hero lived. Human nature in these ages is indebted
> to him for its best portrait (*Works*, XII, 253–254).

Milton's perception of "a purer ideal of humanity" swayed Emerson and caused him to place Milton above Shakespeare as a man and
guide to the higher life for the human race.

In native genius, Milton falls short of Shakespeare and still more
so of the ideal. "Milton was too learned, though I hate to say it,"
Emerson confesses. "It wrecked his originality. He was more indebted to the Hebrew than even to the Greek" (*Journals*, III, 328).
And in the essay "The Poet," Emerson says that Milton is "too liter-

ary" when compared to the ideal poet. He has great native genius, to be sure, but much of his power results from his tremendous learning; for that reason, "His fancy is never transcendent, extravagant" as is Shakespeare's (*Works*, XII, 274). Even so, he was "marked by nature for the great Epic Poet" (*Journals*, I, 71), and he stands out "among so many perverse and partial men of genius" as one in whom "humanity rights itself"; "his virtues are so graceful that they seem rather talents than labours" (*Works*, XII, 262). Despite his great learning, Milton is still a "poet by nature," though not in the same untutored, spontaneous way that Shakespeare is.

When compared with the function of the ideal poet as a representative man, Milton's attempt to live up to the noble ideals he wrote about gave to his actions a nobility worthy of the poet as a man of action. Not only did Milton believe in a greater good for all men—"His opinions on all subjects are formed for man as he ought to be, for a nation of Miltons" (*Works*, XII, 272)—but he tried to lead men to a better world through his actions as well as in his writings. "It was plainly needful," Emerson says, "that his poetry should be a version of his own life, in order to give weight and solemnity to his thoughts; by which they might penetrate and possess the imagination and the will of mankind" (*Works*, XII, 277). Milton is more nearly representative than Shakespeare in the threefold nature of Man Thinking—action, reflection, and expression— and his work represents not only man in his own age but the highest concept of man in all ages.

As a man of Beauty, Milton is not the supreme artist Shakespeare is; his creative imagination is not so free and spontaneous. But Milton's search for truth and goodness creates a solemn beauty that is enduring, though it is without Shakespeare's magical quality. Spontaneous joy and cheerfullness are lacking in the beauty that Milton creates, for his aim is different: he "tasked his giant imagination and exhausted the stores of his intellect for an end beyond, namely, to teach" (*Works*, XII, 277), whereas Shakespeare was content to create beauty to entertain.

In artistry, Milton does not approximate the ideal as nearly as does Shakespeare. In depth and profundity of ideas he equals Shakespeare, if he does not actually surpass him, but in poetic form he is "too literary"; he does not permit his ideas to dictate the form.

> How much one person sways us, we have so few [Emerson says]. The presence or absence of Milton will very sensibly affect the result of human history. . . . [but] to-morrow a new man may be born, not indebted like Milton to the Old, and more entirely dedicated than he to the New, yet clothed like him with beauty. (*Journals*, VI, 141).

Milton, then, is too bound by literary convention and theological tradition to develop fully his potential as a free artist. His is too often form imposed upon thought and not thought dictating form. Even so, Milton rivals Shakespeare in the art of expression:

> His mastery of his native tongue was more than to use it as well as any other; he cast it into new forms. He uttered in it things unheard before. Not imitating but rivalling Shakespeare, he scattered, in tones of prolonged and delicate melody, his pastoral and romantic fancies; then, soaring into unattempted strains, he made it capable of an unknown majesty, and bent it to express every trait of beauty, every shade of thought . . . (*Works*, XII, 260–261).

Finally, Milton's power of transcendency is great, perhaps equal to that of Shakespeare, primarily because of what he said rather than how he said it. *Paradise Lost* goes on the same bookshelf as the Bible because of its great ethical character and because it has the power to lead men to that higher and richer life through its presentation of truth, goodness, and beauty in divinely inspired poetry.

Like the youth presented at the end of the essay "Illusions," Emerson in his pursuit of the ideal poet found himself in a cloudland alone with a lofty and unapproachable ideal, but then occasionally "the air clears and the cloud lifts a little" and there were Shakespeare and Milton and a few others of the great poets of history. However, in Emerson's imagination there were still unfilled seats in this hall of the liberating gods, and he kept waiting for other poets to arrive and fill them.

CHAPTER FIVE

Emerson on his Contemporaries

NEAR THE END OF THE ESSAY "The Poet" (1844), Emerson said, "I look in vain for the poet whom I describe. . . . If I have not found that excellent combination of gifts in my countrymen which I seek, neither could I aid myself to fix the idea of the poet by reading now and then in Chalmer's collection of five centuries of English poets" (*Works*, III, 37–38). He continued the search the remainder of his life and read new poets with anticipation of the arrival of the poet who would be the "liberating god" he had envisioned. Near the end of his life, he selected poems that had been his favorites over the years and published them in the anthology *Parnassus*.[1]

With the absolute standard of the ideal always in mind, Emerson generally applied a more realistic relative standard to his contemporaries. He used the great poets of history (Shakespeare and Milton, for example) as a yardstick by which he judged contemporary poets. He called the great poets "true" poets and "eternal men," because they rose above their time and place and achieved a measure of the ideal; those poets of his own century who did not meet this measure he spoke of as "contemporary men." In many instances his estimates of early nineteenth-century English and American poets have proved accurate.

Those English poets about whom Emerson recorded opinions

are Shelley, Byron, Coleridge, Scott, Keats, Wordsworth, and Tennyson.[2] In "Thoughts on Modern Literature," published in *The Dial* (1840), Emerson attempts to look steadily at the contemporary Romantic poets and give a considered opinion of them. He notes that the "poetry and speculation of the age" have led to a "new consciousness of the one mind" and resulted in an "insatiable demand for unity." He finds the age subjective but with a "Feeling of the Infinite," both of which had "deeply colored the poetry of the period." This "love of the vast," Emerson attributes to German thought; imported into France and thence England, this attitude "finds a most genial climate in the American mind" (*Works*, XII, 318).

It is difficult to understand why Emerson, the admirer of Plato, found so little to admire in Shelley, the most "Platonic" of the English Romantics. Emerson first mentions Shelley in his journals in 1837 and laments the "frantic passions" and "violent colorings" of the "modern" Byrons and Shelleys (*Journals*, IV, 324). In "Thoughts on Modern Literature," Emerson writes:

> Shelley, though a poetic mind, is never a poet. His muse is uniformly imitative; all his poems are composites. A good English scholar he is, with ear, taste and memory; much more, he is a character full of noble and prophetic traits; but imagination, the original, authentic fire of the bard he has not. He is clearly modern. . . . his lines are arbitrary, not necessary.[3]

Although Emerson was not impressed at first with Shelley's *Defence of Poetry*, he read it a second time, "with more love," at Margaret Fuller's insistence.[4] Emerson defended Shelley's character when the *North American Review* and others were exceedingly antagonistic.[5] Though some of his friends read and admired Shelley, Emerson noted in his journal in 1844: "Shelley is wholly unaffecting to me. I was born a little too soon: but his power is so manifest over a large class of the best persons, that he is not to be overlooked." But Emerson could not bring himself to become enthusiastic about Shelley's poetry. Years later, in a letter to James H. Stirling, he praises Shelley for aspiration and "heroic character" but doubted that he was "the poet." "Excepting for a few well known lines about a cloud and a skylark, I could never read one of his hundred pages," Emerson eventually concludes.[6] Shelley, in short, is "contemporary," not "eternal."

Emerson preferred Byron to Shelley, although he was troubled by Byron's personal life.[7] As a boy he had found *Childe Harold* exciting, but by 1846 he could announce, "Byron is no poet: what did he know of the world and its law and Lawgiver?" Finally, in the preface to *Parnassus*, Emerson devotes a paragraph to Byron, reiterating most of the charges he had previously made—lack of serious appreciation of nature, "famine of meaning," "the sublime of schoolboy verse"—and concludes that Byron's talent is "partial"; he has no lofty aim, despite his rare sense of rhythm, "unmatched felicity of expression, a firm ductile thread of gold." Emerson questions whether Byron's brilliant gift of song will "retain for another generation the charm it had for his contemporaries." Byron also was not "eternal" in Emerson's estimation.[8]

Estimating Scott as a poet presented a different kind of a problem. A boyhood favorite, both as poet and novelist,[9] Scott was the cause of no misgivings about his personal life as Byron was to Emerson. But in Emerson's mature judgment, Scott did not reflect the "feeling of the Infinite" Emerson commends in Keats and Shelley. The popularity of Scott's historical and antiquarian poetry did not sway the mature Emerson, who said, "poetry needs little history" (*Journals*, VII, 318). "They praise Scott," he says, "for taking kings and nobles off their stilts and giving them simple dignity, but Scott's grandees are all turgid compared with Shakspear's" (*Journals*, III, 327). Emerson called *The Lay of the Last Minstrel* a "paste jewel" and said in *English Traits* that Scott produced "a rhymed traveller's guide to Scotland" (*Works*, V, 255–256).

But the memory of boyhood pleasures received from Scott's works mellowed somewhat Emerson's judgment over the years. In "Remarks" at the centennial of Scott's birth in 1871, Emerson pays tribute to Scott's charm:

> . . . we still claim that his poetry is the delight of boys. But this means that when we reopen these old books we all consent to be boys again. . . . Critics have found them to be only rhymed prose. But I believe that many of those who read them in youth . . . will make some fond exception for Scott as for Byron (*Works*, XI, 463–464).

Scott, he continues, was "without any ambition to write a high poem after the classic model" and his "strong good sense saved him from the faults and foibles incident to poets,—from nervous egotism, sham modesty or jealousy." Altogether, then, Scott was definitely "contemporary," because his "antique superstitions" were not representative of his time.[10]

Emerson had even less to say about Keats than he did about Shelley. In "Thoughts on Modern Literature," he attributes to Keats the "feeling of the Infinite," though he places him with Coleridge and Shelley as "too subjective." *Hyperion* evidently appealed to Emerson since he quotes from it at least twice and includes four selections from the poem in *Parnassus*. In "Poetry and Imagination," Emerson says that some poets are raised above themselves by inspiration and cites Keats' *Hyperion* as an example. Finally, in a letter in 1868 to James H. Stirling, Emerson says that "Keats had poetic genius, though I could well spare the whole Endymion" (*Letters*, VI, 19).[11] That genius was not developed; consequently, Emerson could not place Keats alongside the great poets.

Coleridge's poetry seems to have made little impression on Emerson, although he was acquainted with it.[12] In view of his high regard for Coleridge's prose and the quality of his mind, Emerson's disregard of Coleridge's poems is difficult to understand. Emerson calls *The Ancient Mariner* a modern antique and warned young poets about such fabrications. He mentions specifically no others of Coleridge's poems.[13]

Wordsworth, whose tall shadow falls across so much of Emerson's speculation about the poet and poetry, presented to Emerson the most complex problem; his poetry contained some of the most appealing ideas, but his style annoyed Emerson. The long time that Emerson took to make up his mind about Wordsworth is justified perhaps by the high place he eventually gave him.

In his youth, Emerson scorned Wordsworth's poetry. In 1826 he complained of Wordsworth's "mystic and unmeaning verses," written "on a theory" (*Letters*, I, xxxiii–xxxiv), a typical reaction in the United States and England during the first quarter of the century.[14] Emerson is displeased by Wordsworth's "modern poetry" which "mauls the moon and waters and bulrushes," objects in nature which Milton and Shakespeare would touch gently, Emersons says. Wordsworth is like the medieval alchemists and astrologers who attempted "to extort by direct means the principles of life, the secret substance of matter from material things" (*Journals*, II, 233). In 1828 Emerson finds *The Excursion* "metaphysical and evanescent" and severely criticizes the style: "Milton," he claims, "would write it off in unpremeditated manuscript and lay it up as a block to be hewn and carved and polished," but "would as soon have hanged himself as publish it as it stands" (*Journals*, II, 236).[15]

Emerson eventually came to see, however, that Wordsworth was "a man of great power and ambition," but he quarrels with his "Ode to Duty," saying, "If he had cut in his Dictionary for words, he could hardly have got worse" (*Journals*, II, 535). But when Emerson began to consider a career of writing, he examined Wordsworth's poetry more carefully and gradually changed his mind; probably his reading of Coleridge's commentary made clearer to him what Wordsworth was attempting to do.[16] Consequently, by the time Emerson went to Europe to seek inspiration, Wordsworth was one of the great men whom he sought out. He was not impressed with the man personally, finding Wordsworth's spouting of his verses somewhat ludicrous. But he reminded himself that he was in the presence of a poet and listened.

The conversion was not immediate nor complete, however. In 1835 Emerson says that Wordsworth "writes ill, weakly, concerning his poetry, talks ill of it, and even writes other poetry that is very poor" (*Journals*, III, 535). Later in that same year, however, he finds more to commend than to dispraise: "It is the comfort I have in taking up those new poems of Wordsworth, that I am sure here to find thoughts in harmony with the great frame of nature, the placid aspect of the Universe. I may find dulness and flatness, but I shall not find meanness and error" (*Journals*, III, 560). Although he continued to find Wordsworth sometimes "garrulous and weak," (*Journals*, IV, 246), he also found that he "gives us the image of the true-hearted man, as Milton, Chaucer, Herbert do" (*Journals*, IV, 356).

In his first published estimate of Wordsworth, Emerson reveals his respect for the English poet's ability. In "Thoughts on Modern Literature" in *The Dial* (1840), Emerson says:

> The fame of Wordsworth is a leading fact in modern literature, when it is considered how hostile his genius at first seemed to the reigning taste, and with what limited poetic talents his great and steadily growing dominion has been established. More than any poet his success has been not his own but that of the idea which he shared with his coevals, and which he has rarely succeeded in adequately expressing. The Excursion awakened in every lover of Nature the right feeling. . . . It was nearer to Nature than anything we had before. . . . More than any other contemporary bard he is pervaded with a reverence of somewhat higher than (conscious) thought. There is in him that property common to all great poets, a wisdom of humanity . . . (*Works*, XII, 320–321).[17]

In his journal for that same year, Emerson declares, "Wordsworth has done as much as any living man to restore sanity to cultivated society" (*Journals*, V, 393). And he wrote to Margaret Fuller in 1842 about the "good sense" of "that pauper poem" (*Letters*, III, 74).[18] Perhaps Emerson was pleased to find his own poems connected with Wordsworth's in a scathing review in the *North American Review* in 1847.[19]

By the time of Wordsworth's death in 1850, Emerson was apparently completely convinced of his greatness. That year brought much commentary in the magazines and new editions of Wordsworth's works; *Harper's Magazine* spoke of him in connection with Milton.[20] Then, in 1852, when a fund was being raised to erect a memorial to Wordsworth, Emerson contributed and said in a note accompanying his contribution that Wordsworth was the "solitariest and wisest of poets" and was the only man among his countrymen "who has not in any point succumbed to their ways of thinking and has prevailed." [21]

In *English Traits* (1856), Emerson still quarrels with Wordsworths' "want of grace and variety, want of due catholicity and cosmopolitan scope," but praised him as the only one in his time who had "treated the human mind well, and with absolute trust." He called "The Ode on Intimations of Immortality" "the high-water mark which the intellect has reached in this age" (*Works*, V, 298). In the late 1860's Emerson read "with delight" a criticism in the *London Reader* which maintained that Wordsworth was the greatest poet since Milton (*Journals*, X, 68), and shortly thereafter he says, "Wordsworth is manly, the manliest poet of his age"

(*Journals*, X, 267–268). Praise of Wordsworth continued during Emerson's last years, and finally in the preface to *Parnassus* (in which the number of Wordsworth's poems is exceeded only by those from Shakespeare), Emerson sketches Wordsworth's reputation over the years, noting his persistence in the face of tremendous opposition. Emerson concludes that Wordsworth "is really a master of the English language; and his best poems evince a power of diction that is no more rivalled by his contemporaries than is his poetic insight. But his capital merit is, that he has done more for the sanity of his generation than any other writer" (*Preface*, pp. viii–ix).[22] The wheel had come full circle.

Emerson's changing opinion of Wordsworth is unusual; he usually made up his mind about writers much sooner. By his standards Wordsworth met the test of the great poets, ranking just below Milton. Wordsworth attained this high place because he was simply and profoundly concerned with life; he "treated the mind well"; he restored nature to its rightful place in poetry; he wrote the only modern "essay" on immortality in the famous "Ode"; and he was "the manliest poet of his age." This final judgment of Wordsworth is the result of a more thorough consideration than Emerson gave to any other nineteenth-century poet. Only Tennyson commanded almost as much of Emerson's attention.

Emerson's many commendations of Tennyson's metrical ability might be cited as proof of a higher regard for poetic form than he is usually said to have. Conversely, this talent of Tennyson's was Emerson's chief criticism—"metres" without the "metre-making argument." Emerson recognized an exceptional gift in Tennyson from the beginning, and John O. Eidson credits Emerson with helping to establish Tennyson's reputation in America:

> Nearly every step of advancement in his [Tennyson's] fame before 1842 can be traced to a member of the so-called Transcendental School. . . . Although he could never make up his mind about Tennyson and never praised him superlatively, Ralph Waldo Emerson in those early years did more than any other single person to make Tennyson known in America. Emerson owned a copy of *Poems, Chiefly Lyrical* as early as December, 1831, and when in 1833 he visited England, he brought back with him a copy of the 1833 *Poems*. Lowell and other Harvard men first

read Tennyson's poems in these books, and with that reading their
enthusiasm for Tennyson began.[23]

In 1838 Emerson attempted to persuade an American publisher to
reprint Tennyson's poems but was unsuccessful. About that time,
Emerson records in his journal that he had read the second volume
of Tennyson's poems, "with like delight to that I found in the first
and with like criticism." He found Tennyson "drenched" in
Shakespeare but with his "own humor, and original rhythm, music
and images" (*Journals*, IV, 411).[24]

Immediately after he saw the new edition of Tennyson's poems
in Boston in 1842, Emerson began a series of entries on Tennyson in
his journal (*Journals*, VI, 218, 243–244, 286–287, 465). He doubts
that there is enough taste in England to do justice to "Ulysses"; he
praises highly the delicate and forceful tones and rhythms of the
poems; he concludes that Tennyson is a master of meter. But Emerson also has his doubts: Tennyson lacks "one great heroic stroke";
he reveals the "misfortune of the time"; and he may not be a great
poet.[25] Then, in "Europe and European Books" in *The Dial* (1842),
Emerson devotes much space to Tennyson. He speaks of his elegance, wit, and subtlety, his rich fancy, metrical skill, and independence of "any living master," but concludes that he "wants
rude truth" and is "too fine." Furthermore,

> Tennyson's compositions are not so much poems as studies in
> poetry, or sketches after the styles of sundry old masters. He is
> not the husband who builds the homestead after his own neces-
> sity. . . . but a tasteful bachelor who collects quaint staircases and
> groined ceilings. We have no right to such superfineness. We
> must not make our bread of pure sugar (*Works*, XII, 371).

Significantly, Emerson does not mention *The Princess*, although
American periodicals were generally laudatory after its publication in 1848 and were influential in swaying British critical opinion
to Tennyson's favor.[26] Perhaps Emerson still felt that Tennyson
wanted a subject. And Emerson felt that Tennyson had not found
it in the work that brought him the laureateship. Emerson's well-
known comment is "Tennyson's *In Memoriam* is the commonplaces of condolence among good Unitarians in the first week of

mourning. The consummate skill of the versification is the sole merit. . . . He is never a moment too high for his audience" (*Journals*, VIII, 163). Not so well known but more illustrative of Tennyson's contemporary reputation is this entry:

> *Fame.* It is long before Tennyson writes a poem, but the morning after he sends it to the *Times* it is reprinted in all the newspapers, and, in the course of a week or two, is as well known all over the world as the meeting of Hector and Andromache in Homer (*Journals*, VIII, 140).

Then, in 1856 in *English Traits*, Emerson offers opinions of poets he had met in England and says of Tennyson:

> Tennyson is endowed precisely in points where Wordsworth wanted. There is no finer ear, nor more command of the keys of language. Color, like the dawn, flows over the horizon from his pencil, in waves so rich that we do not miss the central form. Through all his refinements, too, he has reached the public,—a certificate of good sense and general power, since he who aspires to be the English poet must be as large as London, not in the same kind as London, but in his own kind. But he wants a subject, and climbs no mount of vision to bring its secret to the people. He contents himself with describing the Englishman as he is, and proposes no better (*Works*, V, 257).

In 1858 Emerson notes that Tennyson's poems are the "sublime of magazine poems," suitable contributions "for the *Atlantic Monthly* of the current month, but not classic and eternal." Milton, Emerson adds, would have "raised his eyebrow a little at such pieces" (*Journals*, IX, 152). But with the publication of *Idylls of the King* in 1859, Tennyson redeemed himself, at least in part, in Emerson's estimation: "the long promise to write the national poem of Arthur, Tennyson at last keeps . . ." (*Journals*, IX, 208). Thereafter, Emerson records many compliments for Tennyson's rhythmic power and variety and calls him a brave, thoughtful Englishman. Nevertheless, Tennyson has "far less manly compass" than Wordsworth and is not in the end a great poet. Tennyson glorifies "a perfect English culture, and its petulance" (*Journals*, X, 277).

In the end Emerson could say in 1870 as he had said in 1844, "I look in vain for the poet whom I describe"—with the exception of Wordsworth.

The English poets of the first half of the nineteenth century fare poorly under Emerson's critical gaze, and his American contemporaries measured up even less well. Emerson's opinion of American poetry and American literature in general was somewhat colored by his feeling for his country. Transcendental theory made possible the conviction that great poetry could be produced equally as well in America as in Europe, despite the lack of tradition. When intuition is made the primary means of ascertaining truth, tradition and culture become secondary. The individual can find within his own soul the inspiration to create and does not require great libraries and art museums to spur his imagination. Also, Emerson gave "poetic faith" to theories of culture advanced by Victor Cousin, Johann Gottfried Herder, and Thomas Taylor which, when applied to the United States, seemed to indicate that it was geographically situated so as to take advantage of the best cultural traits of both Europe and Asia.[27] Thus, the contemplative character of Asia and the individualism of Europe should meet and blend in the United States located midway between them. Doubtless, also, the popular political theory called "Manifest Destiny" added a "lustre" to Emerson's thinking, although he was opposed to its manifestation. While politicians were agitating for the expansion of the nation, Emerson was agitating for the expansion of the mind, particularly in the field of poetry. "The question is often asked," he says, "Why no poet appears in America?" (*Works*, VIII, 371); Emerson himself was probably the one who most often asked that question. He laments that young Americans of creative ability run away to Europe for inspiration, forgetting for the moment that he had done exactly that himself. In "The Poet" he calls for the "genius in America" with "tyrannous eye" who can use "our incomparable materials"; "America is a poem in our eyes . . . and it will not wait for metres." He repeats his plea in his "Editor's Address" launching the new *Massachusetts Quarterly Review* in 1847 (*Works*, XI, 385–386).[28]

In spite of his continued search, Emerson had less to say in his essays, journals, and letters about American poets than he did about the English. The Americans he did mention include Bryant,

Whittier, Longfellow, Holmes, Jones Very, Ellery Channing, Thoreau, Lowell, and Whitman.[29]

Emerson's first mention of Bryant, in a letter to William Emerson in 1831, indicates that he did not approve of Bryant's going into newspaper work.[30] In 1835, by which time Bryant had published most of his famous poems, Emerson mentions him in connection with Milton and Burns as being responsible for more tolerance and more appreciation of nature in the world (*Journals*, III, 449).[31] In 1838 Emerson wrote to Margaret Fuller that he had seen Bryant in New York and that Bryant's poetry "seems exterminated from the soil not a violet left—the field stiff all over with thistle & teazles of politics" (*Letters*, II, 129–130). It may be this meeting to which Emerson refers in his journal when he says:

> I said to Bryant and to these young people, that the high poetry of the world from the beginning has been ethical, and it is the tendency of the ripe modern mind to produce it. Wordsworth's merit is that he saw the truly great across the perverting influence of society and of English literature... (*Journals*, IV, 425).

Evidently, Emerson did not consider Bryant's poetry of this high character, for in 1846 he lists him along with Robert Browning, Elizabeth Barrett, and Tennyson as "abortive Homers" that "we praise, or try to" (*Journals*, VII, 165).

Almost twenty years later, Emerson jotted down comments on Bryant, probably in preparation for a public statement:

> Bryant has learned where to hang his titles, namely, by tying his mind to autumn woods, winter mornings, rain, brooks, mountains, evening winds, and wood-birds. Who speaks of these is forced to remember Bryant. American. Never despaired of the Republic. Dared name a jay and a gentian, crows also. His poetry is sincere. I think of the young poets that they have seen pictures of mountains, and sea-shores, but in his that he has seen mountains and has the staff in his hand (*Journals*, X, 76–77).

These notes appear to be the draft of a longer piece written for the Bryant Festival in New York in 1864, in which Emerson probably took part (*Journals*, X, 80).[32]

His sincere, balanced mind has the enthusiasm which perception of Nature inspires ... give him twice his power; he did not parade it, but hid it in his verse. . . . [He] has contrived to levy on all American Nature and subsidized every solitary forest and Monument Mountain in Berkshire or the Katskills, every waterfowl, every partridge, every gentian and goldenrod, the prairies, the gardens of the desert, the song of the stars, the Evening Wind,— has bribed every one of these to speak for him, so that there is scarcely a feature of day and night in the country which does not —whether we will or not—recall the name of Bryant. This high-handed usurpation I charge him with, and on the top of this, with persuading us and all mankind to hug our fetters and rejoice in our subjugation (*Journals*, X, 80–82).[33]

This summary of Bryant's poetry contains high praise for the treatment of nature, although Emerson does not mention, significantly, any connection with Wordsworth, who, in Emerson's opinion, had restored nature to poetry. Nor does Emerson say anything about other elements he expected in great poetry. Clearly Bryant is not to be placed alongside the great poets.

Longfellow as a poet seems to have impressed Emerson but little. In view of their long association as friends and fellow-members of the Saturday Club, Longfellow's part in Emerson's *Journals* is surprisingly small—only three entries. The first of these concerns Longfellow's *Voices of the Night*, his first collection of verse. Lamenting the state of modern poetry, Emerson asks, "But how shall I find my heavenly bread in Tennyson? or in Milnes? in Lowell? or in Longfellow? Yet Wordsworth was mindful of the office" (*Journals*, VII, 163–164). In the several letters between Emerson and Longfellow, there is some guarded commentary on Longfellow's poetry. In 1855 Emerson wrote to congratulate Longfellow on *Hiawatha*:

I find this Indian poem very wholesome; sweet and wholesome as maize; very proper and pertinent for us to read, and showing a manly sense of duty in the poet to write. The dangers of the Indians are, that they are really savage, have poor, small sterile heads, —no thoughts. . . . And I blamed your tenderness now and then, as I read, in accepting a legend or a song, when they had so little to give. I should hold you to your creative function on such occasions. But the costume and machinery, on the whole, is [*sic*] sweet and melancholy, and agrees with the American landscape.

... I found in the last cantos a pure gleam or two of blue sky, and learned then to tax the rest of the poem as too abstemious (*Letters*, I, xlii).

The second entry in the *Journals*, dated 1857, refers to Longfellow's reading of a poem for an occasion at which most of Concord's literary men were present. Emerson says, "The flower of the feast was the reading of three poems, written by our three poets, for the occasion. The first by Longfellow ... all excellent in their way" (*Journals*, IX, 95–96). Holmes and Lowell were the other two poets; Emerson damns all three with faint praise. Significantly, Emerson never refers to Longfellow's great popularity in both England and America by the time of this entry.

The last entry in the *Journals* in which Longfellow's poetry is mentioned concerns the difference between prose and poetry. In poetry, Emerson says, "the mere enumeration of natural objects suffices. Nay, Tennyson is a poet, because he has said, 'the stammering thunder,' or 'the wrinkled sea beneath him crawls'; and Longfellow 'the plunging wave'" (*Journals*, IX, 561). Emerson tended to think of Longfellow and Tennyson together; both suffered from fame and wrote what was expected of them.[34] Longfellow, too, was a great metrical artist; he was "the poet of sentiment." It is apparent that Longfellow's polished, conventional verse and popularized legends did not move Emerson; Longfellow was not the American poet he was seeking.

Emerson saw that Bryant, Longfellow, Whittier,[35] and Holmes[36] —all of his own generation—could not be converted to the transcendental concept of poetry; they were of the past. But there were younger men with the poetic gift who were not traditionbound—Jones Very, Ellery Channing, Henry Thoreau. Emerson turned to them in anticipation; at times he seemed determined to make of them the poets that he thought America called for. There is hardly any other explanation for his patience with Jones Very.

Elizabeth Peabody, also a promoter of genius, discovered Very in 1837. She wasted no time in introducing him to Emerson, who she understood was "at the height of his ardor in his search for American genius."[37] Emerson was impressed by this mystical young man, who "more than others of his contemporaries, seemed ... to rely on intuition, and not on history or social customs as a source of truth." [38] Emerson's *Journals* for 1838 contain many entries concerning this iconoclastic young man such as, "Jones Very charmed us all by telling us he hated us all" (*Journals*, V, 106). To Elizabeth Peabody, Emerson wrote:

> I have been very happy in his visit as soon as I came to understand his vocabulary. I wish the whole world were as mad as he. He discredits himself I think by a certain violence I may say of thought & speech; but it is quite superficial; he is profoundly sane, & as soon as his thoughts subside from their present excited to a more natural state, I think he will make all men sensible of it. . . . At a 'Teacher's Meeting' held at my house, last Sunday Ev[eni]ng I noticed that he passed with some of the company for insane, but all were struck with his insight (*Letters*, II, 171; October 30, 1838).

Meanwhile, Very shocked less sympathetic New Englanders at Harvard and was sent away as a possible mental case. He spent a month in an asylum where he continued work on two essays on Shakespeare which he had already begun. Upon his discharge and return to Salem, he plunged into writing verse and produced some eighty-nine poems in the next seven months, forty-eight of which were printed in the Salem *Observer*.[39] Emerson kept up with his "brave saint" and urged him to publish a volume of poems. Jones Very reluctantly agreed to allow his poems to be put in shape for publication, and during the spring of 1839, prepared the manuscript.[40] The little volume, *Essays and Poems*, published in July, 1839, created no sensation. Margaret Fuller reviewed it in the *Boston Quarterly Review* in January, 1840, and said, in part, ". . . in these little poems, though unfinished in style, and homely of mien, you will find an elasticity of spirit, a genuine flow of thought, and an unsought nobleness and purity almost unknown amid the self-seeking, factitious sentiment." [41] Emerson did not express his views publicly until almost two years later, although he continued to write about Very in his *Journals*. Finally, Margaret Fuller "demanded" that he review the poems for *The Dial*. After apologizing for the tardiness of his review, Emerson speaks of the "pure and kindly temper" of the author and his determination to follow the directions of the Spirit, even "though he should be taxed with absurdity or even with insanity." Then, he guardedly mentions the problem of preparing the poems for the press and the author's objection to changes. Of the poems, Emerson says, ". . . all these verses bear the unquestionable stamp of grandeur." And he adds:

> They are as sincere a literature as the Songs of David or Isaiah. . . .
> These sonnets have little range of topics, no extent of observation,
> no playfulness; there is even a certain torpidity in the concluding
> lines of some of them, which reminds one of church hymns. . . .
> yet are they almost as pure as the sounds of surrounding Nature.[42]

The review shows plainly that Very was not the poet Emerson had been waiting for. But Emerson did not give up his search for promising young men, for in the meantime he had found one who was less mystical and who showed promise—William Ellery Channing.

The great amount of commentary on Ellery Channing in Emerson's *Journals* indicates nothing more than a long and intimate friendship with this indecisive member of the Channing family whom Emerson had so long known. Given to ignoring the demands of poetic form, being the victim of spells of aimlessness, and affecting Emerson's own doctrine of self-reliance, Channing nevertheless remained interesting to Emerson, who thought he saw poetic genius which could be developed. In 1840 Emerson wrote enthusiastically to Channing:

> I have seen no verses written in America that have such inward
> music, or that seem to me such authentic inspiration. Certainly I
> prize finished verses, which yours are not, and like best, poetry
> which satisfies eye, ear, heart, & mind. Yet I prize at such a dear
> rate the poetic soul, that where that is present, I can easily forgive
> the license & negligence the absence of which makes the merit of
> mediocre verses . . . (*Letters*, II, 252–253).

Perhaps he thought this suggestion would be sufficient to put Channing on the right track. Emerson was willing to help; he "toiled over Ellery's manuscripts," Ralph Rusk says, "in the hope of getting the somewhat clumsy poet on his literary feet." [43] Then, in a lengthy article called "New Poetry" in *The Dial*, Emerson "introduced the public to the verse of the dreamy, gentle Ellery Channing." [44]

Emerson tried again, without much hope, to maneuver Channing into improving his technique, as this journal entry shows:

> I spoke the other day to Ellery's ambition and said, Think that in so many millions, perhaps there is not another one whose thoughts can flow into music. Will you not do what you are created to do? . . . But Ellery, though he has fine glances . . . is a very imperfect artist, and, as it now seems, will never finish anything. He does not even like to distinguish between what is good and what is not, in his verses, would fain have it all pass for good,—for the best,—and claim inspiration for the worst lines (*Journals*, VI, 46).

In 1842 Emerson wrote to Margaret Fuller, explaining that, despite Channing's productivity "of good verse" which "would content & delight every gentle soul that was not an Editor," in all these verses there was "never a printable poem at all" (*Letters*, III, 102–103).

Among the record of many walks with Channing in 1843, Emerson notes in his *Journals* that Channing's verse should be called "poetry for poets" since it touches "the fine pulses of thought," but the old complaint against the unfinished nature of his verse continues. Channing, he says, "uses a licence continually which would be just in oral improvisation, but is not pardonable in written verses" (*Journals*, VI, 357–359).[45] Nevertheless, Channing published *Poems: Second Series* in 1847, the same year that Emerson published his own volume of poems, and the *North American Review* devoted twenty pages to a scathing review of the works of the master and the pupil. After dismissing Emerson's poems as mystical, obscure, and "not poetry," the reviewer turns to Channing: "one is tempted to exclaim,—why, this is more excellent foolery than the other. His poetry is a feeble and diluted copy of Mr. Emerson's,—not so mystical and incoherent, but far more childish and insipid. The two publications come together very naturally, as cause and effect." [46]

Years later, in 1855, Emerson still complains of Channing's poetry being "painfully incomplete" (*Journals*, VIII, 541), and the next year he said of new poems by Channing, "He has a more poetic temperament than any other in America, but the artistic executive power of completing a design he has not" (*Journals*, IX, 54). The same charge is made in the *Journals* in 1859 and in a letter in 1860. As late as 1871 Emerson tries to justify Channing by saying that "He does not flatter the reader by any attempt to meet his expectations, or to polish his record." And finally, "He will write as he has ever written, whether he has readers or not. But his poems have to me and to others an exceptional value for this reason" (*Journals*, X, 362).

It was difficult for Emerson to admit that his "promising young genius" had not fulfilled his promise. Emerson had walked with Channing, discussed nature with him, toiled in editing for him, even loaned a great deal of money to him; but Channing refused to write anything more than "village symbols." "Somewhat blinded by his loyalty to the man," Rusk says, "he greatly overestimated the value of Ellery's verse." [47] But the world did not, and perhaps Emerson did not either in the final analysis, for he found in Channing's verse no profound concern with life, no chaunting of the time, no "spermatic" words. Channing, also, was not the poet America expected.

At the height of his enthusiasm for discovering promising young poets, Emerson added Thoreau to his group, which already included Very and Channing. Each of these young men presented a different problem in personal relationships, but Thoreau was of the three destined to become Emerson's whitest hope and perhaps his greatest disappointment as a poet. Emerson was assured of Thoreau's poetic gift from the first. In 1838 in the *Journals* (at the beginning of the notes on many walks with Thoreau), Emerson describes a stroll with Thoreau during which they discussed the restraints modern society places on the individual. Intrigued by the force of Thoreau's opinion, Emerson "begged him" to write it out "into good poetry and so clear himself of it" (*Journals*, V, 128–129). Thoreau apparently did write out some of his thoughts in poetry, for Emerson soon writes:

> Last night came to me a beautiful poem from Henry Thoreau, 'Sympathy.' The purest strain, and the loftiest, I think, that has yet pealed from this unpoetic American forest. I hear his verses with as much triumph as I point to my Guido when they praise half-poets and half-painters (*Journals*, V, 241).

In 1839 Emerson writes to his Aunt Mary that "we have Henry

Thoreau here who writes genuine poetry that rarest product of
New England wit," and he notifies Carlyle, "I have a young poet in
this village named Thoreau, who writes the truest verse." [48]

From the beginning of the acquaintance, Emerson admired
Thoreau's independence. "My brave Henry here who is content
to live now," he says, "and feels no shame in not studying any profession, for he does not postpone his life, but lives already,—pours
contempt on these cry-babies of routine and Boston" (*Journals*, V,
208). Emerson imagined that one of such independence must soon
produce poetry that would put Boston straight concerning the real
values in American life. Thoreau attempted to satisfy his friend's
demand for new poetry, for his own journals during 1840–1842
show an active concern with poetry.[49] But Emerson became im-
patient:

> I told Henry Thoreau that his freedom is in the form, but he does
> not disclose new matter. I am very familiar with all his thoughts,—
> they are my own quite originally drest. . . . I said to him what I
> often feel, I only know three persons who seem to me fully to see
> this law of reciprocity or compensation,—himself, Alcott, and
> myself (*Journals*, VI, 74).

Emerson believed that he had planted ideas in Thoreau's mind—or,
more transcendentally, had uncovered them—and he wanted to see
them mature in poetry. His confidence in Thoreau as a poet remained strong, for he again writes Carlyle in 1841 about Thoreau,
"a poet whom you may one day be proud of;—a noble, manly
youth, full of melodies and inventions." [50] Thoreau struggled to
express himself in verse and to put America in his poems.[51] Emerson, auditor and adviser, was pleased, but he demanded more:

> Last night Henry Thoreau read me verses which pleased, if not
> by beauty of particular lines, yet by the honest truth, and by the
> length of flight and strength of wing; for most of our poets are
> only writers of lines or of epigrams. These of Henry's at least
> have rude strength, and we do not come to the bottom of the
> mine. Their fault is, that the gold does not yet flow pure, but is
> drossy and crude (*Journals*, VI, 304).

There was sufficient "gold" for Emerson to print five of the poems in *The Dial* in October, 1842, and still others in the April, 1843, issue. It may be that Emerson's insistence on "pure gold" in Thoreau's poetry led to the "disagreement." Joseph Wood Krutch says, "According to one of Thoreau's statements, he destroyed a considerable body of verse after Emerson had criticized it harshly...." [52]

By 1844 Emerson had decided that Thoreau did not make "his performance much more manifest than that of the other grand promisers" (*Journals*, VI, 515), and he does not refer to Thoreau's poetry after that. It cannot be assumed that Emerson admired Thoreau less because Thoreau gave up poetry and turned to prose. At least Thoreau showed promise in another direction—as Very and Channing did not—and Emerson was willing to help as his efforts to get Thoreau's works published show. If indeed Emerson was partly responsible for Thoreau's turning away from poetry, it should not be forgotten that he was also responsible for publishing for the first time some of the poetry that Thoreau did write.

James Russell Lowell was slightly younger than Very, Channing, or Thoreau and was by birth of the Brahmin class of Boston. When the twenty-one year old Lowell sent Emerson some of his verse in 1840, Emerson wrote, "I heartily thank you for trusting me with your gay verses. If they have not a high poetical merit, they have broad good nature and good breeding." Emerson said that he had sent the poems on to Miss Fuller for consideration for *The Dial*. This letter, pleasing as it must have been to young Lowell, reveals that Emerson did not see evidence of the "American genius" he was looking for in the verse. Nor did he see it in Lowell's first published volume of verse, *A Year's Life* (1840), nor in *Poems* (1844), nor in *Conversations On Some of the Old Poets* (1845). Lamenting the low state of modern poetry in 1846, Emerson mentions Lowell along with other contemporary English and American poets as not furnishing the "heavenly bread" which he seeks (*Journals*, VII, 163–164).[53]

Emerson does not mention Lowell again in the *Journals* until 1857, by which time Lowell had published most of his important poetry and had become professor of modern languages at Harvard. The 1857 entry records a literary gathering, already referred to, at which Lowell read an occasional poem that made no impression on

Emerson (*Journals*, IX, 95–96). In making a census of "American genius" in 1859, Emerson adds "as an afterthought," Rusk says, "Here is Lowell also" (*Letters*, V, 87). The next mention of Lowell occurs in 1862, shortly after the publication of the second series of *Biglow Papers*. Pleased with Lowell's satire of southerners, Emerson says:

> We will not again disparage America, now that we have seen what men it will bear. What a certificate of good elements in the soil, climate, and institutions is Lowell, whose admirable verses I have just read! Such a creature more accredits the land than all the fops of Carolina discredit it (*Journals*, IX, 359).

Then, in 1864, Emerson wrote to Charles Sumner concerning Lowell: "No literary man in the country suggests the presence of so much power as he; with a talent, too, that reaches all classes" (*Letters*, V, 390). It is significant that Emerson uses the word "talent" rather than "genius," for in an analysis of Lowell's poetry a few years later Emerson emphasizes the difference:

> In poetry, tone. I have been reading some of Lowell's new poems, in which he shows unexpected advance on himself, but perhaps most in technical skill and courage. It is in talent rather than in poetic tone, and rather expresses his wish, his ambition, than the uncontrollable interior impulse which is the authentic mark of a new poem, and which is unanalysable . . . and which is felt in the pervading tone, rather than in brilliant parts or lines . . . (*Journals*, X, 267).

Finally, in 1870, Emerson writes to Lowell to acknowledge the gift of a poem, which Rusk thinks is *The Cathedral*.[54] The poem, Emerson declares, "makes a more serious demand on the reader than any poetry we have seen for long." After complimenting Lowell on his versatility, Emerson continues: "I who am always demanding things in the poetry I read am really gratified with that merit in this poem[.] Here are manly thoughts new, & sharply put, all which & singular I read gladly. The expression is not always flowing," Emerson concludes. This qualified praise is about the highest Emerson paid to any contemporary American poet, with the exception of Whitman. But what Emerson does not say is significant; there is, for instance, no indication that he feels that Lowell has captured the "incomparable materials" of the contemporary American scene. In the end, Emerson seems to place Lowell with Longfellow and Tennyson as the writer of exceedingly finished verse, suitable for the readers who gave it wide popularity, but in the final analysis "contemporary" and not "eternal."

Determining Emerson's opinion of Whitman's poetry is the most difficult of all for lack of positive information. Emerson's original enthusiasm for *Leaves of Grass*—which exemplifies better than any other contemporary work the principles advocated in "The Poet" —makes the temptation very great to credit Emerson with a more complete approval of Whitman than he specifically gave.[55]

Emerson's enthusiastic search for American genius had somewhat abated by 1855; eleven years had passed since he had publicly issued his call for the American poet. The sudden appearance of Whitman undoubtedly revived his hope. It seemed to Emerson at the moment that here at last was the genius with "tyrannous eye" who "knew the value of our incomparable materials," such as he had described in "The Poet":

> Our log-rolling, our stumps and their politics, our fisheries, our Negroes and Indians, our boats and our repudiations, the wrath of rogues and the pusillanimity of honest men, the northern trade, the southern planting, the western clearing, Oregon and Texas . . . (*Works*, III, 37–38).

Leaves of Grass, Emerson saw, was full of America; hence, he wrote the famous letter to Whitman, dated July 21, 1855: He finds the poem "the most extraordinary piece of wit and wisdom that America has yet contributed"; he finds great power in the work; he finds "incomparable things said incomparably well" as a result of "large perception"; he finds "the solid sense of the book" a "sober certainty"; he finds it "fortifying and encouraging"; and, finally, he feels like coming at once to pay his respects to a poet "at the beginning of a great career." [56]

Two months later Emerson wrote with equal enthusiasm to James Eliot Cabot:

> Have you seen the strange Whitman's poems? Many weeks ago I

thought to send them to you, but they seemed presently to become more known & you have probably found them. He seems a Mirabeau of a man, with such insight & equal expression, but hurt hard by life & too animal experience. But perhaps you have not read the American Poem? (*Letters*, IV, 531 [September 26, 1855]).

During the two months that had elapsed between these letters, Emerson had time to reread the book, but apparently his opinion had not changed.

Emerson evidently did not anticipate the storm that broke over the "indecency" of *Leaves of Grass*. Perhaps he did not see the connection with his own pronouncement in "The Poet":

> The vocabulary of an omniscient man would embrace words and images excluded from polite conversation. What would be base, or even obscene, to the obscene, becomes illustrious, spoken in a new connection of thought (*Works*, III, 17).

Emerson definitely was not expecting the obscene when he read *Leaves of Grass* for the first time; therefore, he probably was not shocked. He had said that everything was suitable subject matter for poetry when subjected to the poet's thought. He probably read the poem without paying much attention to the implications of its imagery, so dazzled was he by the fact that at last an American poet had sung America in his poems. Thoreau wrote in his journal in 1856, "As for the sensuality in Whitman's 'Leaves of Grass,' I do not so much wish that it was not written, as that men and women were so pure that they could read it without harm." [57] It was soon apparent that Emerson's friends could not.[58] Their reactions may account for the fact that he was hesitant to send Carlyle the book. When he did write Carlyle, after almost ten months, he was apologetic:

> One book, last summer, came out in New York, a nondescript monster which yet had terrible eyes and buffalo strength, and was indisputably American,—which I thought to send you; but the book throve so badly with the few to whom I showed it, and wanted good morals so much, that I never did. Yet I believe now again, I shall. It is called *Leaves of Grass*,— was written and printed by a journeyman printer in Brooklyn, New York, named Walter Whitman; and after you have looked into it, if you think, as you

may, that it is only an auctioneer's inventory of a warehouse, you can light your pipe with it.[59]

The key phrase here is "indisputably American," praise that Emerson gave to no other book in his time. It is clear that Emerson had been promoting the book and was willing to risk it with his highly critical friend, pointing out the major weaknesses which his contemporaries had found—its catalogs and its morality.

Whitman is mentioned next in Emerson's *Journals* in 1856 when Emerson, reflecting the general reaction to *Leaves of Grass*, notes, "Whipple said of the author of 'Leaves of Grass,' that he had every leaf but the fig leaf" (*Journals*, IX, 33). But the next year in a letter to Caroline Tappan, Emerson refers to "Our Wild Whitman, with real inspiration but choked by Titanic abdomen," and as among "the sole producers America has yielded in ten years." [60] Then, in 1859 in "Art and Criticism" Emerson says:

> Yet much of the raw material of the street-talk is absolutely un-translatable into print, and one must learn from Burke how to be severe without being unparliamentary. Rabelais and Montaigne are masters of this Romany, but cannot be read aloud, and so far fall short. Whitman is our American master, but he has not got out of the Fire-Club and gained the *entrée* of the sitting-rooms (*Works*, XII, 285–286).

Although there is much evidence in Emerson's *Journals* that he approved the use of pithy language, he perhaps did not foresee the use of sexual imagery in poetry when he stated that every subject is fit for poetry; such material, if used at all, must be employed obliquely and not in a starkly realistic manner. No theory of realism in art had been advanced at the time, and Emerson can hardly be expected to sanction obvious sexual realism for public consumption. He does not say that Rabelais, Montaigne, and Whitman should not be read. Nor does he say that Whitman would never be acceptable in "sitting-rooms"; in fact, he almost forecasts that he will be.

Four years later, 1863, an entry in the *Journals* states that ". . . one must thank Walt Whitman for service to American literature in the Appalachian enlargement of his outline and treatment"

(*Journals*, IX, 540). A final entry in 1866, made while Emerson was
reading the Welsh bards, says, "I suspect Walt Whitman had been
reading these Welsh remains when he wrote his 'Leaves of Grass' "
(*Journals*, X, 147). Whitman is not mentioned again in writing
until 1872 in two letters to Lidian Emerson, and these references
do not mention his poetry.[61]

Emerson's meager commentary on Whitman's poetry makes it
difficult to ascertain his final opinion; what he does not say is significant, however. First, he never did recant what he said in the
famous letter of welcome; second, he did not, on the other hand,
indicate that Whitman was to be placed alongside Wordsworth as
a great poet of the nineteenth century. From what has been said
about Emerson's demands for the poet in America, it can surely be
said that Emerson found in Whitman more of his own ideas than
in any other poet of the time.[62] It may be that Emerson felt that
Whitman, like his other promising young geniuses, did not fulfill
the promise he originally showed; perhaps he felt that Whitman
should have gone on from creating an "American Poem" to writing
a universal poem. Whitman himself proposed such a project but
never accomplished it.[63]

Concerning the moral issue, Emerson was not as squeamish as is
generally supposed. He defended Shelley's conduct at a time when
very few people in America were capable of such broadminded-
ness; he never allowed Byron's notoriety to interfere with his judgment of Byron's poetry. Of course, he did not include any of Whitman's poetry in *Parnassus*; either he felt that this "new poetry" did
not belong with the old forms from which it so vastly differed, or
more probably Edith Emerson (the real editor) objected.

It cannot be assumed that Emerson's lack of comment on Whitman is entirely a result of the unfavorable reaction of his friends;
nor can it be assumed that Whitman's refusal to alter *Leaves of
Grass* (if indeed Emerson ever attempted to persuade him to do so)
influenced his opinion.[64] There is sufficient evidence that Emerson
did see real value in Whitman's poetry, although he may not have
considered it the highest value. Such a conclusion does not reflect
on either Emerson or Whitman, given Emerson's high standard of
measurement which so few poets met. The fact remains that Whitman's poetry comes nearer to fulfilling Emerson's demands for an

American poet than does that of any other writer, and that no other poem is given that meaningful title "American Poem" and no other American writer so highly complimented for service to American literature.

This survey of Emerson's opinions shows that his expectations for American poetry influenced to a great degree his judgment of American poets. He insisted that American poetry should employ the incomparable materials the new world offered and combine them with the best thought of the past in order to express adequately man in America in the nineteenth century. The new age must be expressed in all its newness as the last and highest development of the mind of man in the long history of mankind. Such an expression appeared to Emerson to be quite possible in America where restraints on the individual were less than they had been heretofore. The new poetry of the new age must be as vital and alive as American life itself, but at the same time its youthful vigor must be solidly based on the same deep thought and artistry that had made great poetry of the past timeless.

CHAPTER SIX

Emerson's Contribution to Poetic Theory

As EMERSON SAID of Shakespeare's being a most "indebted man," so was he in evolving his concept of the nature, function, and art of the poet. His eclectic method permitted him to range far and wide in the philosophy and literature of the Western world (including Arabic poetry) and pick up striking ideas (which he called "lustres") wherever he found them and to rephrase ideas into a pattern that is in effect a system of his own.

Emerson had two standards by which he measured a poet—an absolute standard and a relative one. The absolute standard derived from an ideal that exists in the mind only and that can be only partially approximated by human beings; he says, "when we adhere to the ideal of the poet, we have our difficulties even with Milton and Homer" (*Works*, III, 38). This position led Norman Foerster to state:

> Using a term that Poe abhorred, Emerson demands a 'transcendental' criticism. We must judge books, he says, by absolute standards. . . . Confronted with a new poem, for instance, we are not to ask whether it compares passably with certain good poems that it reminds us of, or even whether it can stand unblushingly beside the works of Homer and Shakespeare and Milton, but whether it justifies itself in relation to the hypothetically supreme poem, the very Sun of poems which outshines even our masterpieces. Nay,

we must be prepared to go still further; for the very Sun of poems is yet but a poem and not essential truth itself—beyond the ideal poem is the Ideal itself, the criterion of all human striving.[1]

The relative standard used the great poets of history (Homer, Shakespeare, Milton, and others) as a yardstick against which lesser poets were measured; "we do not speak of men of poetical talents, or of industry and skill in meter, but of the true poet." The absolute standard, subject to no vagaries of time, place, or history, is conceivable only by transcendental means; the relative standard acknowledges the limitations of time, place, and human capabilities. To put it another way, the *idea* of the omnipotent poet has always existed and will continue to exist in the minds of men; in the course of human history a few great poets have exemplified degrees of the *ideal*, but none has completely approximated it. Emerson frequently mixes these two standards without regard to consistency. He uses the classifications of "contemporary" and "eternal"; "contemporary" refers to poets who do not transcend the limitations of their own time and place, and "eternal" signifies poets who have risen above these limitations to a universality in which inheres a great measure of the ideal. Shakespeare is "eternal," for example, because his native genius defied rules, tradition, and convention in creating an enticing world of the imagination; by contrast Scott and Byron are "contemporary."

Indebted as he was to prior commentary on poets and poetry, Emerson, nevertheless, by the force of his convictions and by the impact of his own style heightened the ancient belief in the sacredness of the poet's profession and added some "lustres" of his own: he enlarged upon the concept of the independence of the poet as artist; he spelled out a broader function for the poet in society; he showed the way toward more inclusive subject matter for poetry; and he phrased a fuller statement of ideals for American poetry.

By making the poet's intuition the test of truth, Emerson frees him from the dominance of literary convention and the past. "Well might then the poet scorn," Emerson says in the poem "The Poet," "To learn of scribe or courier / Things writ in vaster character" (*Works*, IX, 326). Wordsworth had led the way to a greater independence for the poet by insisting that he is a man speaking to men and by advocating greater freedom in subject matter and style. Emerson extends the bounds of theory by making the poet a representative man speaking to all men and by giving primacy to the poet's intuition. From this standpoint, the past and literary tradition become far less important than they had been in poetic theory, especially during the preceding century. They have value for the poet only insofar as they enable him to ascertain those universal elements in the poetry of the past that have enabled it to transcend its own age and live into succeeding ages. The poet sees that modes of poetic expression change even as political and religious forms change, and that the manner of expression that is natural to one age may not be suitable for succeeding ages. Convention, so regarded, is a means of education for the poet; the end toward which he works is a new expression of his own age, and whatever he finds in the past that will assist him is to be regarded as a means. The past, if regarded as sacred and authoritarian because it is the past, thwarts the natural growth and development of the poet's mind.

The eclectic use of the past does not, on the other hand, free the poet from restraint. In the poem "The Poet," the questioning poet is informed by the Chorus of Spirits to look within himself—"Thine own theatre art thou." The Spirits assure him that they and he are governed by the same law—"See, all we are rooted here / By one thought to one same sphere; / From thyself thou canst not flee,— / From thyself no more can we" (*Works*, IX, 319). Thus, the poet is not permitted an irresponsible self-expression, because he is subject to universal laws.

Emerson's emphasis on the poet as a representative man in society extended the duties and responsibilities of the poet beyond the limits of previous theory. Emerson agreed with the Greek belief that the work of the poet is one of the chief means of instilling virtue in man because it opens his eyes to beauty, but he saw that the benefits of the poet's work were likely to be limited to the fortunate few in the Greek world. He saw the same limitations in Renaissance poetic theory in its stress on the poet-patron relationship; he saw that Neo-Classical poetic practices confined the poet to the society of the London coffee houses. He saw that the theories of natural reason as common to all men, of benevolence, and of the perfectibility of man were steps in the right direction; even the primitivism of

Rousseau and the political thinking of Godwin and Paine operated to elevate the concept of the common man. He saw that Wordsworth was the first theorizer to assume that the poet in his function is not a courtier, a town or university wit, or a secluded scholar, but is a man speaking to men. He agreed with Wordsworth that the artificiality of poetry and the superficiality of poets could be done away with only by a return of the poet and poetry to the people. But he also saw that Wordsworth made a distinction between the poet as a man and the people in general, for Wordsworth's theory and practice implied a certain aloofness in the poet, who, though living among the people and writing about them, remains somewhat apart from them.

Emerson narrows the margin of separation, although he does not completely merge the poet and the common man as Whitman later did. The necessary periods of withdrawal are stressed in "The Apology," "Woodnotes," and the poem, "The Poet." The idea serves as a kind of refrain in "Saadi"—"But the poet dwells alone". . . . "Good Saadi dwells alone". . . . "Wise Saadi dwells alone." But the dominant note is that he returns to the world of men because he is a "brother" to the world. Whereas previous theory permitted social and political distinctions even while glorifying the common man, Emerson sees that such distinctions in a classless, democratic society are false. Unwilling to acknowledge complete egalitarianism, however, he insists on a kind of intellectual aristocracy to which the poet belongs, making him superior in degree rather than in kind, depending upon his higher development of faculties common to all men. But this superiority of the poet increases his responsibility to his fellowmen and makes the poet more acutely aware of this responsibility, not to any limited few, but to mankind in general. The poet, therefore, as a man speaking to men and as a truly representative man has a definite and vital place in society as a citizen and artist and as a speaker for all men. He is the personification of the poetic impulse in all men. Thus, the democratization of poets beginning with Wordsworth is furthered by Emerson's theory and is made manifest eventually in Whitman's theory and practice.

Emerson's advocacy of the enlarged function of the poet leads to the broadening of the whole field of subject matter and poetic form. His assumption that everything is suitable subject matter for poetry is a tremendous step forward, especially in advance of eighteenth-century theory which limited the poet by rules governing subject matter and form. The basis for Emerson's new interpretation of subject matter is his belief in a divinely created universe, any part of which shares in the divinity of the Creator and is therefore inherently good, true, and beautiful. The poem "Mithridates" lists elements of nature and man available to the poet. "I cannot spare" anything from "the earth-poles to the Line," Emerson begins; "Everything is kin of mine." As would be expected, he lists beautiful things in nature, but, less characteristically, he includes those that are "wild" and "sharp and slimy" as well. "I will use the world and sift it," he avows, "To a thousand humors shift it." Man similarly will be shown, not just in his nobility, but also "Reputed wrongs and braggart rights, / Smug routine, and things allowed, / Minorities, things under cloud!" These, too, are the stuff of poetry (*Works*, IX, 28–29).

Emerson's belief in the dual nature of man and his conviction that work, when performed with nobility of purpose, has dignity, make the whole range of human activity suitable subject matter. Though he did not follow his own recommendation in the essay "The Poet" and use "things obscene," he does have the Muse instruct Saadi, "Seek not beyond thy cottage wall," but to consider the "gray-haired crones" who gossip before his door; his very servants may be "gods in servile masks" (*Works*, IX, 135). In "Hamatreya" Emerson saw his own neighbors—"Bulkeley, Hunt, Willard, Hosmer, Meriam, Flint"—as examples of man's deception by illusions:

> Earth-proud, proud of the earth which is not theirs;
> Who steer the plough, but cannot steer their feet
> Clear of the Grave.

The earth says,

> 'They called me theirs,
> Who so controlled me;
> Yet every one
> Wishes to stay, and is gone . . .' (*Works*, IX, 35–37).

The smaller, or more humble, the example, the more lasting the impression created.

Emerson's belief that all human experience is fit subject matter for the poet causes him to include science and scientific investigation. Although others of the Romantics were friendly toward science, especially Wordsworth and Shelley, Emerson more eagerly accepted scientific theory and investigation as another revelation of the harmony and beauty of the universe, and he insists that the poet use this specialized knowledge to show the relationship of the law for things and the law for man. He readily adopted the theories of progressive adaptation and evolution as evidence of the upward trend of things, and he fitted them into his doctrine of the spiraling nature of all life. After Uriel announces his circular philosophy that shakes the foundations of orthodoxy, he withdraws in the "sad self-knowledge" that new truths are too blinding for immediate acceptance; but the "forgetting wind" that blew over Paradise did not forever silence the "truth-speaking things" (the "chemic force" and "the speeding change of water") that caused the gods to quake, "they knew not why" (*Works*, IX, 13–15). The famous motto attached to later editions of *Nature*—"And, striving to be man, the worm / Mounts through all the spires of form"—reflects, as Frederic Carpenter says, the theory of evolution "which had been in the air for fifty years before Darwin gave it scientific formulation." [2] A less familiar hint appears in the poem "Bacchus": "And the poor grass shall plot and plan / What it will do when it is man" (*Works*, IX, 126)—a statement that Whitman may well have noticed and remembered. The neglected poem "Wealth" is a summary of advanced thinking about the origin of the world in Emerson's time. It begins with a picture of the "lifeless ball" on which the lichen, "puny seeds of power," abraded rocks over untold ages to "build in matter home for mind." The gradual covering of "The granite slab" and the perishing of "races" to pave the planet "with a floor of lime" left fossils and coal. All is "waste and worthless" until "the wise selecting will . . . out of slime and chaos . . . Draws the threads of fair and fit." The remaining sixteen lines of the poem sketches human history with emphasis on man's inventions:

Galvanic wire, strong-shouldered steam ...
But though light-headed man forget,
Remembering Matter pays her debt:
Still, through her motes and masses, draw
Electric thrills and ties of law,
Which bind the strengths of Nature wild
To the conscience of a child (*Works*, IX, 286).

Rather than regarding scientific investigation and modern invention as negations of the importance of man and God, Emerson saw them as a means for making general laws concrete, thus adding another "lustre" to his optimism for man.

Emerson's statement of goals for American poetry was the most explicit and complete of any made up to his time. He was aware that since the American Revolution there had been demands for an American literature, sometimes in terms of common sense,[3] but, more frequently, as a result of pained reactions to British criticism. Ignoring the literary quarrel between John Bull and Brother Jonathan, Emerson gave a logical explanation of how American poetry could be developed. His belief that the intuition of the individual is the final test of truth and that every soul shared in the creative ability of the Divine denied the necessity of national tradition and poetic convention and made the writing of poetry in America as natural and logical as in Europe. Although he agitated for an American poetry and enthusiastically greeted Whitman's "American Poem," he went far beyond the narrow nationalism characteristic of his age and advocated a universal poetry in America rather than a national poetry as such. To Emerson, truth and poetry were not a matter of national boundaries, although it is true that he was inclined to believe that American democratic society was more favorable to the free development of the poet as a man speaking to men than those societies that valued the individual less. But back of his insistence that American materials be used and that the "American poem" be written, there is always his conviction that the poet should use the materials at hand with such artistic selectivity that only the universal elements emerge. By this method, the poet who captures the spirit of the new and complex America in his poems is well on the way toward transcending national boundaries and creating a universal poetry. This attitude may account for the very few undisputably American references in his poems other than the patriotic and topical ones.[4]

Emerson as theorizer in poetry stands midway between Wordsworth and Whitman. Better than any of his contemporaries, Emerson understood Wordsworth's attempt to democratize poetry by returning it to nature and the people. Emerson fused ideas from Wordsworth with his own Transcendental theories and arrived at the conclusion that man as poet has the ability to harmonize man, nature, and God into a new whole and has the obligation to speak for the poetic impulse in the souls of all men. Whitman made the logical extension and application of Emerson's theory by assuming the role of the divinely-appointed speaker for the American democratic masses. He became the comforter and joy-giver further democratized into the comrade and "elder brother," who embraced in manly love his fellowmen and his nation—ultimately the whole world—and looked forward to the time when poetry would replace vitiated religious forms, and all men would be their own poets. Emerson realized that his theory tended in that direction.

Like the Plotinian "divine aura" circulating throughout the universe, the pure brilliance of Emerson's vision of the ideal poet shines through all that he thought and said about poets and poetry. And near to the source of that overpowering light of the ideal stands the incarnation of it, man as poet. This liberating god was all that Emerson conceived of Plato as being—a great and magnanimous soul into whom poured all streams of thought, East and West, and from whom issued ideas in a fountain of incomparable beauty, flowing forever across the landcape of time. If Emerson himself was primarily a poet as twentieth-century critics tend to view him,[5] then he, consciously or not, may have played the role in nineteenth-century America of a new Plato in a New World. And if his works are a poetic record of the life of the mind,[6] then his occasional glimpses of the transcendent reality, sometimes expressed in words of divine fire, will remain "as new as foam, and as old as rock," for he has told "us how it was with him, and all men will be the richer in his fortune."

Notes

INTRODUCTION

1. Leonora C. Scott, *The Life and Letters of Christopher P. Cranch*, pp. 65–66.
2. *The Complete Works of Ralph Waldo Emerson*, ed. Edward Waldo Emerson. Hereafter cited in the text as *Works*.
3. Norman Foerster, *American Criticism: A Study in Literary Theory from Poe to the Present* and Therman B. O'Daniel, "Emerson As a Literary Critic," *CLA Journal*, VII (1964), 21–43, 157–189, and 246–276. See also Emerson G. Sutcliffe, "Emerson's Theories of Literary Expression," *University of Illinois Studies in Language and Literature*, VIII (1923), 9–143; John B. Moore, "Emerson on Wordsworth," *PMLA*, XLI (March, 1926), 179–192; Jean Gorely, "Emerson's Theory of Poetry," *Poetry Review*, XXII (July–August, 1931), 263–273; John T. Flanagan, "Emerson as a Critic of Fiction," *Philological Quarterly*, XV (January, 1936), 30–45; and Seymour L. Gross, "Emerson and Poetry," *South Atlantic Quarterly*, LIV (January, 1955), 82–94.
4. *The Works of Plato*, ed. and trans. Thomas Taylor.
5. *The Journals of Ralph Waldo Emerson*, ed. Edward Waldo Emerson and Waldo Emerson Forbes. Hereafter cited in the text as *Journals*.
6. See Kenneth W. Cameron, *Emerson the Essayist: An Outline of His Philosophical Development Through 1836* and Cameron's *Ralph Waldo Emerson's Reading*.

7. *The Letters of Ralph Waldo Emerson*, ed. Ralph L. Rusk, III, 47. Hereafter cited in the text as *Letters*.
8. Ralph Waldo Emerson, ed. *Parnassus*.

CHAPTER ONE

1. "Indebted" refers not to borrowing, but rather to the use of ideas innate in the mind.
2. In succeeding stanzas Emerson begs indulgence for his seeming idleness while he listens to what nature has to teach. The concluding stanza, addressed to a farmer-neighbor, says that after the farmer gathers his harvest, the land yields a "second crop" which Emerson the poet gathers "in a song."
3. The terminology "partial" and "complete" may come from Proclus' commentary on Plato, especially his attempt to explain the doctrine of reminiscence in the *Phaedrus*. The "partial" soul, Proclus says, is that one which is still hampered by the body and does not depend entirely on spiritual powers. The "complete" soul abnegates the body entirely and is governed exclusively by spirit. Emerson, always reluctant to go to the extremes of Neo-Platonic asceticism, characteristically adopts only part of the concept, or rather the terminology of it.
4. See Frederick I. Carpenter, *Emerson Handbook*, pp. 217–218.
5. Thomas Taylor in his notes to the *Cratylus* (*The Works of Plato*, V) cites Proclus extensively, especially his comment on the gods. Proclus speaks of the triad—Jupiter, Neptune, and Pluto. Jupiter (Jove), the father, represents being; Neptune represents power; Pluto represents intellect; likewise, he says that this triad is composed of that which is essential, vital, and intellectual.
6. Cf. the essay "Beauty" (*Works*, VI, 279–306). Also, Coleridge (*Biographia Literaria*, II, 256–257): "What is beauty? It is, in the abstract, the unity of the manifold, the coalescence of the diverse; in the concrete, it is the union of the shapely (*formosum*) with the vital. In the dead organic it depends on regularity of form . . . in the living organic it is not merely regularity of form, which would produce a sense of formality; neither is it subservient to anything besides itself. It may be present in a disagreeable object, in which the proportion of the parts constitute a whole; it does not arise from association . . . it is not different to different individuals and nations, as has been said, nor is it connected with the ideas of the good, or the fit, or the useful. The sense of beauty is intuitive, and beauty itself is all that inspires pleasure without, and aloof from, and even contrarily to, interest."

7. Because of Emerson's fondness for the symbolic figure of the circle, the "centre" has a special significance. He was familiar with the lengthy commentaries of the Neo-Platonists on the mystical significance of the circle. Thomas Taylor (*Works of Plato*, I, xxvii), in commenting on Plato's concept of *the good, the one*, says, "As the monad and the centre of a circle are images from their simplicity of this greatest of principles, so likewise do they perspicuously shadow forth to us its casual comprehension of all things. For all numbers may be considered as subsisting in the monad, and the circle is the centre. . . ."

8. In *Poems*, Vol. IX of the *Complete Works*, Edward Waldo Emerson included in "Appendix" the long piece entitled "The Poet," about which he said: "This poem, called in its early form 'The Discontented Poet, a Masque,' was begun as early as 1838, probably earlier. It received additions through several years and was much improved, but Mr. Emerson never completed it." He thinks that the poem was written "parallel, so to speak, with the lectures on the same theme" and that the original title was discarded as the ideas emerged that finally became the essay "The Poet." "The poem truly pictures," he says, "his own method of seeking inspiration, sitting under the pines in Walden woods by day and walking alone under the stars by night,—listening always" (pp. 500–501).

9. *Preface to Lyrical Ballads, The Poetical Works of William Wordsworth*, ed. E. De Selincourt, II, 394.

10. The doctrine of "the flowing" or flux Emerson found in Plato, where it is attributed to Heraclitus. The image was appealing to Emerson, but he characteristically altered it. Whereas the Heraclitean "river philosophy" implies a constant flowing at a slowly descending level, as the river, Emerson associated it with the upward tendency of the spiral. In "The Poet," he says, ". . . within the form of every creature is a force impelling it to ascend into a higher form" (*Works*, III, 20). Vivian C. Hopkins, *Spires of Form*, pp. 2–3, says: ". . . spirit is energy projected from intellect, constantly flowing through matter and rendering it more alive; and implicit in this Plotinian idea of 'the flowing' is the concept of upward ascension (later made explicit for Emerson by the evolutionary theory of natural science). Thus Emerson's own term of 'the spiral' admirably hits the combination of circular movement with upward progress which is the heart of his aesthetic."

11. Wordsworth in the *Preface* says: "If the labours of Men of science should ever create any material revolution, direct or indirect, in our condition, and in the impressions which we habitually receive, the Poet will sleep then no more than at the present; he will be ready to follow the steps of the Man of science. . . . The remotest

discoveries of the Chemist, the Botanist, or Mineralogist, will be as proper object of the Poet's art as any upon which it can be employed . . ." (*The Poetical Works*, II, 397).

12. See Harry H. Clark, "Emerson and Science," *Philological Quarterly*, X (July, 1931), 224–260; also, Joseph W. Beach, "Emerson and Evolution," *University of Toronto Quarterly*, III (July, 1934), 474–497.

13. J. W. H. Atkins, *Literary Criticism in Antiquity*, I, 116.

14. *The Complete Works of Sir Philip Sidney*, ed. Albert Feuillerat, III, 20.

15. *The Complete Works of Percy Bysshe Shelley*, eds. Roger Ingpen and Walter E. Peck, VII, 112.

16. Thomas Carlyle, *Critical and Miscellaneous Essays*, II, 237.

17. Emerson was, of course, familiar with Plato's description of the "divine fury" as it appears in the *Phaedrus*, 244, *Ion*, 533–534, and Book X of the *Republic*. In a note to the *Ion*, Thomas Taylor paraphrases Jamblichus' distinction between "enthusiasm" and "inspiration." Taylor then concludes, "The spirits which from the divinities excite and agitate men with divine fury, expell all human and physical motion, nor are their operations to be compared with our accustomed energies; but it is requisite to refer them to the gods, as their primary causes" (*Works of Plato*, V, 46).

18. That is, great accomplishments through concentration of power defy time and make achievements appear miraculous (See *Works*, I, 128 ff.).

19. *Biographia Literaria*, II, 258.

20. Taylor regarded this dialogue as a study in etymology. *The Dialogues of Plato*, ed. B. Jowett. 3d ed., London: 1892, I, 258–259, says: "In the Cratylus he [Plato] gives a general account of the nature and origin of language, in which Adam Smith, Rousseau, and other writers of the last century, would have substantially agreed." And, "Plato is a supporter of the Onomatopoetic theory of language; that is to say, he supposes words to be formed by the imitation of ideas in sound."

CHAPTER TWO

1. Emerson found in Plato's *Symposium* the suggestion of the "eternizing" quality of poetry, that is, that great deeds of men were memorably preserved in the works of poets. Also, Horace, concerned with the relationship of the poet to society, advocated the creation of an exalted poetry that would be of service to the state (J. W. H. Atkins, *Literary Criticism in Antiquity*, II, 62 ff).

Renaissance commentators made much of the importance of the poet to the ruler and the state. Puttenham states that since the days of Alexander, poets have been the associates, confidants, advisers, and inspirers of rulers (*The Arte of English Poesie*, eds. Gladys D. Willcock and Alice Walker, pp. 6–18 *passim*).

2. Emerson also said of Shakespeare: "The Pilgrims came to Plymouth in 1620. The plays of Shakespeare were not published until three years later. Had they been published earlier, our forefathers, or the most poetical among them, might have stayed to read them" (*Works*, XI, 453).

3. Emerson was doubtless familiar with the ancient argument concerning the superiority of poetry over history and philosophy. Traditionally, Aristotle had been interpreted as contending that poets were the equals—if not the superiors—of Plato's philosopher-kings, in rejoinder to Plato's ban, or at least regulation, on the type of poetry that might be produced in the Republic. Sir Philip Sidney explains that Plato actually excluded only the abuse of poetry, not poets themselves and cites Aristotle to prove that the poet is superior to the philosopher and historian as teacher (J. E. Spingarn, *A History of Literary Criticism in the Renaissance*, p. 268). For Emerson, Milton exemplified the ideal of the poet as a guide to a better political and moral state for man. Emerson says (*Journals*, I, 71), "What a grand man was Milton! so marked by nature for the great Epic Poet that he was to bear up the name of these latter times. In 'Reason of Church Government urged against Prelaty,' written while young, his spirit is already communing with itself and stretching out its collosal proportions and yearning for the destiny he was appointed to fulfill." Near the end of his life, Emerson remarks (*Parnassus*, Preface, vii) in apology for not including *Paradise Lost* in his collection of favorite poems: "Milton's 'Paradise Lost' goes so surely with the Bible on to every book-shelf, that I have not cited a line. . . ."

4. *The Poetical Works of William Wordsworth*, ed. E. De Selincourt, II, 396.

5. *The Poetical Works*, II, 400.

6. *The Complete Works of Percy Bysshe Shelley*, ed. Roger Ingpen and Walter E. Peck, VII, 137.

7. *Symposium*, 186, 187: ". . . in music there is the same reconciliation of opposites. . . . harmony is composed of differing notes of higher and lower pitch which disagreed once, but are now reconciled by the art of music; for if the higher and lower notes still disagreed, there could be no harmony,—clearly not. For harmony is symphony, and symphony is agreement . . ." (Jowett translation, I, 556–557).

8. "Let the victory fall where it will, we are on that side. And the

knowledge that we traverse the whole scale of being, from the centre to the poles of nature, and have some stake in every possibility, lends that sublime lustre to death, which philosophy and religion have too outwardly and literally striven to express in the popular doctrine of the immortality of the soul. The reality is more excellent than the report. Here is no ruin, no discontinuity, no spent ball. The divine circulations never rest nor linger. Nature is the incarnation of a thought, and turns to a thought again, as ice becomes water and gas. The world is mind precipitated, and the volatile essence is forever escaping again into the state of free thought. Hence the virtue and pungency of the influence on the mind of natural objects, whether inorganic or organized. Man imprisoned, man crystallized, man vegetative, speaks to man impersonated. That power which does not respect quantity, which makes the whole and the particle its equal channel, delegates its smile to the morning, and distils its essence into every drop of rain. Every moment instructs, and every object; for wisdom is infused into every form" (*Works*, III, 195–196).

9. John S. Harrison, *The Teachers of Emerson*, p. 205.

10. Emerson goes on to list a number of daring poetic expressions or concepts as examples of language that has a liberating effect on the mind. A paraphrase of the list follows: Aristotle defines space as an immovable vessel in which things are contained; Plato defines a line as a flowing point and a figure as a bound of solid. Socrates speaks of incantations as "beautiful reasons" which cure maladies of the soul. Plato calls the world an animal, and Timaeus calls man a heavenly tree. Orpheus speaks of hoariness as "that white flower which marks extreme old age." Proclus calls the universe the statue of the intellect. St. John compares the falling stars to a fig tree casting her untimely fruit.

11. *Works*, IX, 446–447. E. W. Emerson's note states: "It does not appear in what year Mr. Emerson first read in translation the poems of Saadi. . . . he adopted his name, in its various modifications, for the ideal poet, and under it describes his own longings and his most intimate experiences." In the *Journals* (1843) Emerson says in a brief biography of Saadi that a host of angels descended with "salvers of glory" for Saadi because he had written a stanza of poetry that pleased God.

CHAPTER THREE

1. Bliss Perry, *Emerson Today*, p. 87, says, ". . . his enormously wide reading in poetry furnished him with examples of the most diver-

gent theory and practice. In this field, as elsewhere, he has no theory to inculcate: he simply communicates an enthusiasm for poetry and interprets it with an insight denied to the system-makers."

2. Said Saadi, "When I stood before
   Hassan the camel-driver's door,
   I scorned the fame of Timour brave;
   Timour, to Hassan, was a slave.
   In every glance of Hassan's eye
   I read great years of victory,
   And I, who cower mean and small
   In the frequent interval
   When wisdom not with me resides,
   Worship Toil's wisdom that abides.
   I shunned his eyes, that faithful man's,
   I shunned the toiling Hassan's glance."

   In his notes to this section of the poem "The Poet," E. W. Emerson says that Hassan was "without doubt, Mr. Emerson's sturdy neighbor, Mr. Edmund Hosmer, for whom he had great respect. The camels were the slow oxen, then universally used for farmwork, with which Mr. Hosmer ploughed the poet's fields for him" (*Works*, IX, 506).

3. H. D. Gray, *Emerson: A Statement of New England Transcendentalism*, says that statements by Lowell, Holmes, Garnett, and other early commentators were responsible for the impression that Emerson lacked a sense of form; Firkins, Dewey, and some religious writers defended him. Among recent scholars who have defended Emerson are Charles H. Foster, "Emerson as American Scripture," *New England Quarterly*, XVI (March, 1943), 91–105; Robert P. Falk, "Emerson and Shakespeare," *PMLA*, LVI (March, 1941), 532–543; Vivian C. Hopkins, *Spires of Form* (1951); and Hyatt H. Waggoner, *American Poets from the Puritans to the Present*.

4. Atkins, *Literary Criticism in Antiquity*, I, 54–55, says: "Among the outstanding principles of art revealed in his [Plato's] writings none is however more illuminating than that principle of organic unity which he regarded as one of the primary conditions of art. The most familiar of his pronouncements on this point occurs in the *Phaedrus*, where he states that 'every discourse . . . ought to be constructed like a living creature, having a body of its own as well as a head and feet, and with a middle and extremeties also in perfect keeping with one another and the whole.' And here, it will be noticed, he requires not only the unity or completeness that is provided by a suitable beginning, middle, and end, but also a unity that is vital in kind, all the parts being related as the parts of a

living organism, so that nothing could be changed or omitted without injury to the whole."

5. As quoted by F. O. Matthiessen, *American Renaissance*, pp. 133–134. Similar expressions of the organic principle appear elsewhere in *Biographia Literaria*: "Nothing can permanently please, which does not contain in itself the reason why it is so, and not otherwise" (II, 9), and the parts of a poem must "mutually support and explain one another" (II, 10).

6. Miss Hopkins, *Spires of Form*, p. 72, explains: "Coleridge whom Emerson began to read in 1830, and whose influence continued during his productive years, supplied Emerson with the application of organic form to literature." In the essay "Poetry and Imagination," some of which was written as early as 1841, Emerson says that in good poetry "the sense dictates the rhythm." He adds, "I might even say that the rhyme is there in the theme, thought and images themselves. Ask the fact for the form. For a verse is not a vehicle to carry a sentence as a jewel is carried in a case: the verse must be alive, and inseparable from its contents, as the soul of man inspires and directs the body . . ." (*Works*, VIII, 54).

7. This passage, originally used in a lecture on The Poet in 1841, echoes the *Ion* in which Plato says that the lyric poets "tell us that they bring songs from honeyed fountains, culling them out of the gardens and dells of the Muses; they, like the bees, winging their way from flower to flower" (Jowett, *The Dialogues of Plato*, I, 502).

8. Miss Hopkins, *Spires of Form*, p. 137, says, "The principal lack in Emerson's concept of form is the gap which exists between the intuition in the artist's mind and its transference to objective matter. Although this lack may not be explained away, it can be better understood in the light of Emerson's distrust of the principle of imitation."

9. Throughout Emerson's works there are many references to words as actual things. This concept may owe something to both history and theology. Atkins, *English Literary Criticism*, p. 88, says, "One of the great commonplaces of antiquity had been the power of Logos, of reason as it expresses itself in speech. . . ." He points out that medieval writers had a superstitious reverence for words, such as Roger Bacon's belief that all miracles had been performed by means of words and that all words in the Bible had manifold powers (pp. 132–133). Emerson, of course, was familiar with the discussion of words in Plato's *Cratylus*. Cameron, *Emerson the Essayist*, I, 278, cites Sampson Reed, who, he believes, "had a definite influence upon Emerson's theory of poetry," as using the expression "words make one with things." He also notes that Emer-

son wrote a sermon in 1831 entitled "Words are Things" (I, 416). Cameron assumes (I, 295 ff) that Emerson was familiar with Oegger's theory of an original language of nature before the fall of man and that Emerson draws on this theory for information in the chapter on "Language" in *Nature*.

In the essay "Inspiration," Emerson says, "What is best in literature is the affirming, prophesying, spermatic words of men-making poets" (*Works*, VIII, 294). In "Poetry and Imagination," he declares, "It cost the early bard little talent to chant more impressively than the later, more cultivated poets. His advantage is that his words are things . . ." (*Works*, VIII, 57).

10. The entry reads: "The language of the street is always strong. . . . I feel too the force of the double negative, though clean contrary to our grammar rules. And I confess to some pleasure from the stinging rhetoric of a rattling oath in the mouth of truckmen and teamsters. How laconic and brisk it is by the side of a page of the *North American Review*. Cut these words and they would bleed; they are vascular and alive; they walk and run. Moreover they who speak them have this elegancy, that they do not trip in their speech. It is a shower of bullets, whilst Cambridge men and Yale men correct themselves and begin again at every half sentence."

11. Emerson, of course, never used such language. He was, as Allen says (*American Prosody*, p. 96), a "blazer of trails," and Whitman's following him on this particular trail caused a great deal of controversy. Emerson continued to admire pungent speech; in "Art and Criticism" (1859), he says: "Montaigne must have the credit of giving to literature that which we listen for in barrooms, the low speech,—words and phrases that no scholar coined; street-cries and war-cries; words of the boatman, the farmer and the lord; that have neatness and necessity, through their use in the vocabulary of work and appetite, like the pebbles which the incessant attrition of the sea has rounded" (*Works*, XII, 295–296). And in his poem "Monadnoc" he refers to the "four-score or hundred words" of the "hardy English root" that comprise the vocabulary of New England farmers (*Works*, IX, 66–67).

12. This use of words in their ultimate meanings is no easy task. "Homer's words," Emerson declares, "are as costly and admirable to Homer as Agamemnon's victories are to Agamemnon" (*Works*, III, 7), and he quotes Goethe as saying, "Each *bon mot* of mine has cost a purse of gold" (*Works*, III, 104).

13. In "Poetry and Imagination" (*Works*, VIII, 13–14), Emerson asserts, ". . . a good symbol is the best argument, and is a missionary to persuade thousands. The Vedas, the Edda, the Koran are each remembered by their happiest figures. There is no more welcome gift to men than a new symbol. That satiates, transports, converts

them. They assimilate themselves to it, deal with it in all ways, and it will last a hundred years."

14. Emerson charges that mystics mistake an accidental and individual symbol for a universal one and attach a static meaning to that symbol. As an example, he cites Jacob Behmen's constant use of "morning redness" as a symbol for truth and faith. He adds, "And the mystic must be steadily told,—All that you say is just as true without the tedious use of that symbol as with it. Let us have a little algebra, instead of this trite rhetoric,—universal signs, instead of these village symbols,—and we shall both be gainers."

15. The kinship of this idea to Berkeleian idealism is obvious. Yet for Emerson it is a "lustre" rather than a dogma, for he does not deny the existence of matter. Rather he uses the idealistic concept of the creative ability of the mind to emphasize his theory that every natural fact is symbolic of a spiritual fact, and that the correspondence between fact and thought is the important thing. Miss Hopkins, *Spires of Form*, p. 7, says: "Through the concept of correspondence, which affirms that the phenomenal world and man's spirit are meant to be united, Emerson establishes the rationale of his aesthetic. Man reacts to the spirit which exists in phenomena, but he also infuses such objects as stars and stones with the subtle fluid of his own spiritual insight. Just as in the natural world Emerson takes the dualistic rather than the monistic position, recognizing the actuality of tree, flower, and bird, so in art does he admit the reality of the artifact. But his fascination with the idealism expressed by Berkeley and the Hindu philosophers confirms his native disposition to place greater value upon spirit than upon matter."

16. A little earlier Emerson had written in his *Journals* (VII, 158), "Bardic sentences how few! . . . If I now should count the English Poets who have contributed aught to the Bible of existing England and America sentences of guidance and consolation which are still glowing and effective—how few! Milton, Shakespeare, Pope, Burns, Young, Cowper, Wordsworth—(what disparity in the names! yet these are the authors) and Herbert, Jonson, Donne."

17. Garrod (*New England Quarterly*, III, 18–19), says: "Of aphorisms and apothegm he is one of the greatest masters in literature; the equal, I think, of Seneca. . . . His prose, like his verse, is best, no doubt, in what is properly called the sentence, in what the Latins, I mean, understood by the word *sententia*, in the moral aphorism, in that kind of epigram which, in so far as it aims rather at the affections than at the mind, deserves some better name."

18. Cameron, *Emerson the Essayist*, I, 417, says that Emerson preserved in manuscript a large collection of proverbs and epigrams.

19. In *Journals* V, 304–305, Emerson refers to a letter he wrote to S. G.

Ward in which he discusses the difference between the first impression of a poem and a painting. By the picture, the eye "is astonished or delighted once for all, and quickly appeased, whilst the sense of a verse steals slowly on the mind and suggests a hundred fine fancies before its precise import is settled."

20. "Cold allegory makes us yawn, whatever elegance it may have" (*Journals*, VIII, 40). "Nature never draws the moral, but leaves it for the spectator. Neither does the sculptor, nor the painter, nor the poet" (*Journals*, VII, 190).

21. "There are also prose poets. Thomas Taylor, the Platonist, for instance, is really a better man of imagination, a better poet, or perhaps I should say a better feeder to a poet, than any man between Milton and Wordsworth" (*Works*, VIII, 50).

22. The concept is, of course, as old as Aristotle. Atkins says (*Literary Criticism in Antiquity*, I, 82), Aristotle infers that "the term 'poet' included all imaginative artists in words, whether working in prose or verse; and in this identification of poetry with imaginative literature generally, Aristotle was followed by more than one later theorist." The Neo-Platonists and Thomas Taylor regarded Plato not only as the "prince of philosophers" but "the first of poets" (*Works of Plato*, I, 438). Sidney believed that "One may be a *Poet* without versing, and a versifier without Poetrie" (*Complete Works*, III, 27). Wordsworth was convinced that there was no "*essential* difference between the language of prose and metrical composition" (*Poetical Works*, II, 392). Shelley declared that ". . . the popular division into prose and verse is inadmissible in accurate philosophy," and that "Plato was essentially a poet . . ." (*Complete Works*, VII, 113–114). Emerson questions, "Between poetry and prose must the great gulf yawn ever, and they who try to bridge it over be lunatics or hypocrites?" (*Journals*, V, 96).

CHAPTER FOUR

1. Robert P. Falk, "Emerson and Shakespeare," *PMLA*, LVI (March, 1941), 532–543. Falk says that Emerson generally follows Coleridge in romantic idolatry of Shakespeare, but with "Yankee restraint."

2. Thoreau came closer than Emerson in placing Shakespeare in the proper historical relationship. Thoreau says (*Journals*, I, 465–466): "After all, we draw on very gradually in English literature to Shakespeare, through Peale and Marlowe, to say nothing of Raleigh and Spenser and Sidney. We hear the great tone already sounding to which Shakespeare added a serener wisdom and

clearer expression. Its chief characteristics of reality and unaffect-
ed manliness are there. The more we read of the literature of those
times, the more does acquaintance divest the genius of Shakespeare of the in some measure false mystery which has thickened
around it, and leave it shrouded in the grander mystery of day-
light. His critics have for the most part made their [*sic*] contemporaries less that they might make Shakespeare more."
3. In *Representative Men*, Emerson says (*Works*, IV, 210), "Some able
and appreciating critics think no criticism on Shakespeare valu-
able that does not rest purely on the dramatic merit; that he is
falsely judged as poet and philosopher. I think as highly as these
critics of his dramatic merit, but still think it secondary."
4. Richard C. Pettigrew, "Emerson and Milton," *American Literature*,
III (March, 1931), 47.

CHAPTER FIVE

1. Ralph Waldo Emerson, ed., *Parnassus*.
2. Browning, Arnold, Swinburne, Clough, Rossetti, and other Victor-
ian poets are not included because Emerson had little or nothing
to say about them. For example, he mentions Browning only three
times (*Journals*, VI, 286–287; VII, 165–166; and VIII, 455), never
favorably. Oswald Doughty, *Dante Gabriel Rossetti*, p. 450, says
that when the poet-painter William Bell Scott asked Emerson "if
the Americans had not cared for Rossetti's poetry, the philosopher
of the 'oversoul' replied: 'Yes, we scarcely take to the Rossetti
poetry; it does not come home to us; it is exotic; but we like
Christina's religious pieces.' "
3. This statement is transcribed almost verbatim from a passage in the
Journals for 1839 (V, 344); the last line continues, "But all his
lines are arbitrary, not necessary, and therefore, though evidently
a devout and brave man, I can never read his verses."
4. Margaret Fuller wrote to Emerson in April, 1840, "I wish you would
read his Essay 'The defence of Poetry' . . ." (*Letters*, II, 291).
Emerson replied May 28, 1840, "I have looked into the Shelley
book not yet with much satisfaction[.] It has been detained too
long[.] All that was in his mind is long already the property of the
whole forum and this Defence of Poetry looks stiff & academical"
(*Ibid.*, II, 299). On June 7, 1840, he wrote her again, "I have read
Shelley a little more with more love" (*Ibid.*, II, 305).
5. Julia Power, *Shelley in America in the Nineteenth Century*, p. 53.
6. *Works*, VIII, 25. E. W. Emerson says in a note to this statement:
"Mr. Emerson always heard with impatience the praise of the

poems of Shelley, with the exception of a few which he included in his collection, *Parnassus.*" These poems are "The Cloud" and "The Skylark."

7. In an early journal entry concerning Byron's death, Emerson says that although Byron was "a man of dreadful history . . . the light of sublimer existence was on his cheek . . . Wit, argument, history, rhapsody, the extremes of good and ill,—everything was to be expected from his extraordinary invention" (*Journals*, II, 4–5).

8. *Parnassus*, Preface, p. ix. It is interesting to note that Emerson prints thirty-three poems by Byron in this collection as compared to two of Shelley's and forty-three of Wordsworth's.

9. Rusk, *Letters*, I, xxxv, says: "Among the major Romantic writers Scott is mentioned or quoted more frequently than any but Wordsworth. . . . Doubtless Emerson read more from Scott than any other novelist, and we come upon sufficient evidence that he remembered both novels and poems."

10. In the Preface to *Parnassus*, p. iv, Emerson says, "Scott was . . . an accomplished rhymer . . . admirable chronicler, and master of the ballad. . . ." He prints twenty-seven of Scott's poems in that collection.

11. In "Manners" (*Works*, III, 119–155), Emerson quotes ten lines of *Hyperion* in connection with his discussion of aristocracy, and in "The Sovereignty of Ethics" (*Ibid.*, X, 183–214), he quotes two lines from the same poem. Margaret Fuller in a letter to Emerson in 1840 says, "I see Shelley in his letter to Gifford makes the same distinction in favor of Keats' Hyperion over his other works that you did" (*Letters*, II, 291).

12. Cameron, *Emerson the Essayist*, I, 166, shows that Emerson borrowed from the Boston Athenaeum, January, 1830, Coleridge's *Sibylline Leaves*, which contains almost all of his poetry written between 1793 and 1817. He also shows (*Ibid.*, I, 149–169) that Emerson borrowed from the Boston Library Society Coleridge's *Poetical Works* four times in 1839–1840.

13. Rusk thinks that he may allude to two of them in letters.

14. Annabel Newton, *Wordsworth in Early American Criticism*, p. 60 ff., points out that Wordsworth was little known in America before 1824, although a reprint of *Lyrical Ballads* appeared in 1802. What published criticism there was generally followed the lead of the hostile *Edinburg Review.*

15. The *North American Review* agreed. In 1824 it printed an article attacking Wordsworth's "defects," and in 1829 it referred to his "mistaken system" (Newton, *Wordsworth*, pp. 67–68).

16. Frank T. Thompson, "Emerson's Indebtedness to Coleridge," *Studies in Philology*, XXIII (Jan , 1926), 55–56, says, ". . . but for Coleridge's work as a critic he might never have accepted Words-

worth's Nature poetry." Rusk, however, feels that Emerson's Aunt Mary may have been influential. In 1826 she wrote Emerson commenting that the rare things in Sampson Reed's *Observations on the Growth of the Mind* were borrowed from Wordsworth. "Presently Emerson," Rusk says, "showed a change of heart" (Letters, I, xxxiv).

17. Other American periodicals were discovering Wordsworth about the same time. The *New York Review* in 1839 devoted a seventy-seven page review and exposition to the ode on immortality, and in 1841 the *Southern Literary Messenger* printed an article on it (Newton, *Wordsworth*, p. 124).

18. Perhaps Emerson would have been amused to know that Wordsworth did not find such good sense in his own Essays. In 1841 Wordsworth says, "Our Carlyle and he [Emerson] appear to be what the French used to call Esprits forts. . . . Our two present Philosophers, who have taken a language which they suppose to be English for their vehicle, are verily 'Par nobile Fratum,' and it is a pity that the weakness of our age has not left them exclusively to the appropriate reward [,] mutual admiration. Where is the thing which now passes for philosophy at Boston to stop?" (As quoted by Markham L. Peacock, Jr., *The Critical Opinions of William Wordsworth*, p. 253.)

19. LXIV (1847), 402–434. The reviewer says that Wordsworth has the "questionable honor" of leading the way to an exaggerated concern with nature and that Emerson's poetry is of the same "school."

20. Newton, *Wordsworth*, p. 154.

21. Newton, *Wordsworth*, p. 162.

22. Both Margaret Fuller and James Russell Lowell agree that Wordsworth is the greatest poet of the period. (See Miss Fuller's "Modern British Poets," *Art, Literature, and Drama*, pp. 99–109, and Lowell's long biographical and critical essay, "Wordsworth," *The Writings of James Russell Lowell*, IV, 354–415.) Poe, however, gives first place to Tennyson. In the early "Letter to B." Poe treats Wordsworth with scorn. Even if the "Letter to B." does not represent Poe's mature attitude toward Wordsworth as has been claimed in Margaret Alterton and Hardin Craig, *Edgar Allan Poe*, New York: 1935, p. 524, the absence of extensive comment on Wordsworth in later years indicates that Poe saw in his poetry little to agree with his own theory of poetry.

23. John Olin Eidson, *Tennyson in America: His Reputation and Influence from 1827 to 1858*, pp. 5–6.

24. Eidson, *Tennyson in America*, p. 33.

25. Eidson, *Tennyson in America*, p. 35. "Particularly significant is the fact that the first American edition consisted of fifteen hundred to

two thousand copies; whereas, the English publisher was willing to risk only eight hundred" (p. 38). "Emerson's estimate of Tennyson," Eidson adds (p. 41), "remained little changed after 1842."

26. Eidson, *Tennyson in America*, p. 68.
27. Cameron, *Emerson the Essayist*, I, 415, says that Emerson was familiar with Herder's *Outlines of a Philosophy of the History of Man* (1803); "Herder," Cameron explains, "had been among the first to show the relationship between climate and character." Harrison, *The Teachers of Emerson*, pp. 265–266, comments: "This association of the sacred writers of the East with Plato and the Platonists may have arisen from Emerson's adoption of the critical attitude of Cousin. That French philosopher. . . . denominated Asia the land whose fundamental character is unity; where all the elements of human nature lay enveloped indistinct within each other; while Greece was the land in which these same elements were developed and separated. It is a distinction that recalls Emerson's statement that Asia is the country of unity, while Greece is the land of culture and intellectual freedom."

Taylor translated a section of Book V of Plato's *Laws*: ". . . this ought not to be concealed from us, that there is a great difference in places, with respect to producing men of a more or less excellent character; and that laws should be established accommodated to such places." Taylor added a note which reads: ". . . a change is produced in different nations from the places themselves which each inhabit; from the temperament of the air, and from habitude to the heavens; and still more from spermatic reasons. But they most especially differ according to the gregarious government of the Gods, and the diversities of inspective guardians; through which . . . you will find colours, figures, voices, and motions changed in different places" (*Works of Plato*, II, 141–142).

28. One paragraph reads: "We harken in vain for any profound voice speaking to the American heart, cheering timid good men, animating the youth, consoling the defeated, and intelligently announcing duties which clothe life with joy, and endear the face of the land and sea to men. It is a poor consideration that the country wit is precocious, and, as we say, practical; that political interests on so broad a scale as ours are administered by little men with some saucy village talent, by deft partisans, good cipherers; strict economists, quite empty of all superstitions."

29. These poets, with the exception of Whittier and Holmes, have been selected for examination because Emerson's comments on them are extensive enough to obtain a representative opinion. Whittier and Holmes have been included because they were major literary figures of the time. Not included are the numerous minor poets listed in George Willis Cooke's *The Poets of Trans-*

cendentalism (1903). Several of these poets were known to Emerson personally, but his brief comments on them are limited almost entirely to his letters to Margaret Fuller concerning the publication of poetry in *The Dial*.

30. "Why had not Cullen the grace to go back to corn & potatoes & spit at 'dirty and dependent bread
    From pools & ditches of yᵉ Commonwealth.'
    I talked much to his brother Cyrus about your man's folly in leaving poetry, and hope yᵗ it mt [*sic*] reach him that his Verses have ardent and all unprejudiced admirers" (*Letters*, I, 325).

31. The passage reads: "If Milton, if Burns, if Bryant, is in the world, we have more tolerance, and more love for the changing sky, the mist, the rain, the bleak, overcast day, the indescribable sunrise and the immortal stars. If we believed no poet survived on the planet, nature would be tedious."

32. E. W. Emerson's note says "it seems probable" that Emerson took part in the celebration.

33. Emerson reprints eight of Bryant's poems in *Parnassus*.

34. Odell Shepard, *Henry Wadsworth Longfellow*, p. xli, says Longfellow's poems "were meant not for a few highly cultivated readers but for all. Communication meant more to him than self-expression. He did not seek what is now called 'originality,' but rather he sought to be a good spokesman. . . . He won his public in the recognized way, by phrasing its own thoughts and beliefs. . . ."

35. Emerson's opinion of Whittier's poems may only be guessed at, for nowhere in his *Journals* or elsewhere does he comment upon them. Rusk speculates (*Letters*, I, xlii) that "Whittier . . . appealed for direct action a little too impatiently and insistently to suit Emerson's philosophical mood."

36. Emerson apparently cared little for humorous or light verse of the type that Holmes was noted for. Seven of Holmes' poems appear in *Parnassus*, probably more in recognition of a long friendship than for any other reason.

37. William I. Bartlett, *Jones Very: Emerson's "Brave Saint,"* p. 45.

38. Bartlett, *Jones Very*, p. 48.

39. Bartlett, *Jones Very*, p. 58.

40. Bartlett, *Jones Very*, pp. 66–67, says, ". . . in answer to Emerson's suggestions for altering phrases or lines in his poems or even for careful proofreading, [Very] again insisted that his works were not his but those of the Spirit, and hesitated to perform an action implying such irreverence. Emerson had little patience with a judgment which confused Spirit itself with the human expression of it."

41. Bartlett, *Jones Very*, p. 103.

42. Bartlett, *Jones Very*, p. 106. Carlos Baker, "Emerson and Jones

Very," *New England Quarterly*, VII (March, 1934), 90–99, says, "Emerson observed in himself a conflict between masculinity and feminity, between reliance on self and reliance on God, between initiative and resignation to fate, between fanciful and pragmatic application. . . . He recognized Very as his weak side, the oriental (passive) side" (p. 96). Emerson included two of Very's poems in *Parnassus*.

43. *Ralph Waldo Emerson*, p. 254.

44. Rusk, *Ralph Waldo Emerson*, p. 277.

45. Thoreau wrote in his journal: "I think it would be a good discipline for Channing, who writes poetry in a sublimoslipshod style, to write Latin, for then he would be compelled to say something always, and frequently have recourse to his grammar and dictionary" (*The Heart of Thoreau's Journals*, Odell Shepard, ed., p. 100.)

46. "Nine New Poets," LXIV (1847), 402–434. The reviewer attacks the "school of which Mr. Emerson and Mr. Channing are the brightest ornaments," and accuses the members of "puling raptures," "indiscriminate and idolatrous worship" of the outward universe, and "heathenish philosophy." "Mr. Wordsworth," he adds, "has the questionable honor of leading the way to this exaggerated and fantastic manner, and of perverting the love of nature from its proper tendency to see everywhere 'the unambiguous footsteps of God' into a mere cover and pretense of some paltry dreams drawn from Pythagorean philosophy" (p. 420).

47. Rusk, *Ralph Waldo Emerson*, p. 298. Eight of Channing's poems are included in *Parnassus*.

48. *The Correspondence of Thomas Carlyle and Ralph Waldo Emerson*, ed. Charles E. Norton, I, 256.

49. *The Journals of Henry D. Thoreau*, eds. Bradford Torrey and Francis H. Allen. Reprinted 1949. See I, 114–115 (1840); I, 274–275, 278, 288, 289 (1841); I, 357 (1842). Carl Bode, ed., *Collected Poems of Henry Thoreau*, p. ix, says: "For several years after graduation from 'Cambridge College' he considered himself a practicing poet. Much of the large amount of verse he mentions writing has not come down to us, but what is left still forms a far larger body than a glance through his collected works might lead anyone to think."

50. *Correspondence of Carlyle and Emerson*, I, 335.

51. The poem "With Frontier Strength Ye Stand Your Ground" (*Collected Poems*, p. 47) has a kind of national sweep that reminds one of Whitman. "Our Country" (*Ibid.*, p. 134) makes an even greater sweep of the geography and polyglot races of America. "I Seek the Present Time" (*Ibid.*, p. 165) stresses the importance of the present over the past.

52. Joseph W. Krutch, *Henry David Thoreau*, p. 261. The Emerson-

Thoreau correspondence, edited by F. B. Sanborn, *Atlantic Monthly*, LXIX (May, 1892), 557–596, and (June, 1892), 736–753, shows some evidence of a possible "disagreement." In a letter of September 8, 1843, Emerson says that he objects to some "mannerisms" "an old charge of mine" in Thoreau's poem "Winter Walk," which he was editing for *The Dial*. "By pretty free omissions, however," he continues, "I have removed my principal objections" (p. 593). Thoreau replies on September 14 that he is agreeable to the editing (p. 594). After the poem was printed, however, Thoreau writes on October 17, "I see that I was very blind to send you my manuscript in such a state. . . . There are some sad mistakes in the printing." And in the same letter Thoreau severely criticizes Emerson's "Ode to Beauty," printed in the same issue of *The Dial*.

Four of Thoreau's poems appear in *Parnassus*.

53. Poe, on the other hand, predicted in 1842 that Lowell would become a "genius of the highest rank" (*The Complete Works of Edgar Allan Poe*, XI, 125), and said in his review (*Ibid.*, XI, 243–249) of *Poems* (1844) that these poems would put Lowell "at the head of American poets."

54. *Letters*, VI, 100. Seven of Lowell's poems appear in *Parnassus*.

55. The personal relationship of Emerson and Whitman has been discussed by John B. Moore, "The Master of Whitman," *Studies in Philology*, XXIII (March, 1926), 77–89; Foerster, *American Criticism*, p. 168; C. F. Gohdes, "Whitman and Emerson," *Sewannee Review*, XXXVII (March, 1929), 79–93; Spiller and others, *Literary History of the United States*, I, 481–482.

56. Louis Untermeyer, ed., *The Poetry and Prose of Walt Whitman*, pp. 963–964.

57. Thoreau, *Journals*, IX, 149.

58. Rusk, *Letters*, IV, 520–521, says: "Emerson's later silence on the subject of *Leaves of Grass* was, I believe, due in no small degree to the astonishment and dismay of a number of his personal friends. Thoreau was, as we know, an exception, though he too made reservations. And there were other exceptions, but adverse opinion was strong. J. P. Lesley, Philadelphia, Nov. 25, 1855, said he had examined the 'profane & obscene' *Leaves of Grass* and thought the author a pretentious ass without decency; then he had been confronted with a newspaper clipping containing what purported to be a letter of respect and gratitude to that same author over the name of one whom, of all American thinkers, he most revered. He asked now for Emerson's confirmation of his own immediate assertion that the quoted letter was not genuine but only a malicious jest. Bennett H. Nash wrote from Old Cambridge, Mar. 25,

1856, apparently surprised at learning that his kinsman had read the book; he asked whether it was, then, worth reading and what were Whitman's antecedents. Even so clearheaded a critic as Lowell never, he said in 1863, had looked into *Leaves of Grass* farther than to satisfy himself that it was a "solemn humbug" and, since his attention had been called to its more objectionable features, would take care to keep it out of the way of Harvard students."

59. *Correspondence of Carlyle and Emerson*, II, 251.
60. *Letters*, V, 87. Emerson says of Thoreau (*Journals*, IX, 401), "Perhaps his fancy for Walt Whitman grew out of his taste for wild nature."
61. While on a lecture tour, Emerson wrote, ". . . tonight at my second lecture [in Baltimore] Walt Whitman presented his picturesque person . . . Whitman bringing Sumner's invitation that I should come to him tomorrow" (*Letters*, VI, 193); five days later he wrote, ". . . Sumner . . . sent a messenger (no less than Walt Whitman) to invite me to his house . . ." (*Ibid.*, VI, 195).

    Charles J. Woodbury in *Talks with Ralph Waldo Emerson*, reports that Emerson once said to him that *Leaves of Grass* "is a wonderful book you must certainly read. It is wonderful. I had great hopes for Whitman until he became a Bohemian" (pp. 62–63).
62. Some of the basic ideas in Emerson's concept of the poet which are reflected in Whitman are: the divine nature of man; the doctrine of intuition; the poet as man speaking to men; the poet as seer and prophet—Whitman's poet-prophet-statesman; the poet as representative man—in Whitman, egalitarian democracy; the poet as comforter and joy-giver—Whitman's elder brother and comrade; the creative process as "Nature passed through the alembic of man"—Whitman's "swallowing soul"; the poet as the best "scientist"; the concept of organic form; self-reliance; optimism; reconciliation of opposites; respect for the past but not veneration.

    Some of Emerson's suggestions that Whitman developed more fully are: everything is suitable subject matter for poetry, including heretofore excluded material; bare lists of words may be poetic—Whitman's catalogs; the poet should tell "how it is with him"; the new age requires a new expression; American materials should be used in poetry; the times and social circumstances should be included in contemporary poetry; ideas should dictate the form of poetry; and every man may become his own poet.
63. In the 1876 preface, Whitman says, "It was originally my intention, after chanting in 'Leaves of Grass' the songs of the body and existence, to then compose a further, equally needed volume, based on

those convictions of perpetuity and conservation which, enveloping all precedents, make the unseen soul govern absolutely at last" (*Prose Works*, p. 281).

64. In a note to "Persian Poetry" (*Works*, VIII, 421), E. W. Emerson says, ". . . he welcomed Whitman's free and New World singing (rather, however, in its promise than in its result), but, as that author has told us, and with pride that he did not yield to the friendly urgency, did his best to persuade him to keep his work always within the decencies."

CHAPTER SIX

1. Norman Foerster, *American Criticism: A Study in Literary Theory from Poe to the Present*, pp. 54–55.

2. Frederic I. Carpenter, *Ralph Waldo Emerson, Representative Selections*, p. xxxiii.

3. Bryant's lectures on poetry, given in 1826, were not published until 1884, and Emerson may not have been acquainted with them. In one of these lectures, "On Poetry and Its Relation to Our Age and Country," Bryant concludes: "I infer, then, that all the materials of poetry exist in our own country, with all the ordinary encouragements and opportunities for making a successful use of them. The elements of beauty and grandeur, intellectual greatness and moral truth, the stormy and the gentle passions, the casualties and the changes of life, and the light shed upon man's nature by the story of past times and the knowledge of foreign manners, have not made their sole abode in the old world beyond the waters. If under these circumstances our poetry should finally fail of rivalling that of Europe, it will be because Genius sits idle in the midst of its treasures" (Tremain McDowell, *William Cullen Bryant*, p. 213).

4. The pine tree urges the poet in "Woodnotes" to create a "nobler rhyme" than his present strains that "Only thy Americans" can read; it sings instead in many languages (*Works*, IX, 53–54). In the unfinished "Fragments on the Poet," appears the native allusion to "A cabin hung with curling smoke, / Ring of axe or hum of wheel" (*Works*, IX, 321). Even the poems with New England settings—"The Rhodora," "Berrying," "Monadnoc," "Musketaquid"—are universal in intent.

5. Stephen E Whicher, ed., *Selections from Ralph Waldo Emerson: An Organic Anthology*, p. xx; Hyatt H. Waggoner, *American Poets from the Puritans to the Present*, pp. 89–114.

6. Stephen E. Wicher, *Freedom and Fate: An Inner Life of Ralph Waldo Emerson*, pp. vii, 28.

Bibliography

BOOKS

Alterton, Margaret, and Craig, Hardin, eds. *Edgar Allan Poe: Representative Selections*, American Writers Series. New York: American Book Co., 1935.

Atkins, J. W. H. *Literary Criticism in Antiquity*. Cambridge: Cambridge University Press, 1934. 2 vols.

Bartlett, William I. *Jones Very: Emerson's "Brave Saint."* Durham: Duke University Press, 1942.

Cameron, Kenneth W. *Emerson The Essayist: An Outline of His Philosophical Development Through 1836*. Raleigh, North Carolina: The Thistle Press, 1945. 2 vols.

Cameron, Kenneth W. *Ralph Waldo Emerson's Reading*. Raleigh, North Carolina: The Thistle Press, 1941.

Carlyle, Thomas. *Critical and Miscellaneous Essays*. London: Chapman & Hall Ltd., 1894. 3 vols.

Carpenter, Frederic I. *Emerson Handbook*. New York: Hendricks House, Inc., 1953.

Carpenter, Frederic. *Ralph Waldo Emerson: Representative Selections*. American Writers Series, New York: American Book Co., 1934.

Coleridge, Samuel T. *Biographia Literaria*, ed. J. Shawcross, Oxford: Clarendon Press, 1907. 2 vols.

Cooke, George Willis. *The Poets of Transcendentalism*. Boston: Houghton, Mifflin & Co., 1903.

Doughty, Oswald. *Dante Gabriel Rossetti*. New Haven: Yale University Press, 1949.

Eidson, John Olin. *Tennyson in America: His Reputation and Influence from 1827 to 1858.* Athens, Georgia: University of Georgia Press, 1943.

Emerson, Ralph Waldo. *The Complete Works of Ralph Waldo Emerson.* Edited by Edward Waldo Emerson. Boston: Houghton Mifflin Co., 1903–1904. Centenary Edition. 12 vols.

Emerson, Ralph Waldo, and Carlyle, Thomas. *The Correspondence of Thomas Carlyle and Ralph Waldo Emerson.* Edited by Charles E. Norton. Boston: James R. Osgood & Co., 1888. 2 vols.

Emerson, Ralph Waldo. *The Journals of Ralph Waldo Emerson.* Edited by Edward Waldo Emerson and Waldo Emerson Forbes. Boston: Houghton Mifflin Co., 1909–1914. 10 vols.

Emerson, Ralph Waldo. *The Letters of Ralph Waldo Emerson.* Edited by Ralph L. Rusk. New York: Columbia University Press, 1939. 6 vols.

Emerson, Ralph Waldo, ed. *Parnassus.* Boston: John R. Osgood & Co., 1875.

Emerson, Ralph Waldo. *Selections from Ralph Waldo Emerson: An Organic Anthology.* Edited by Stephen E. Whicher. Boston: Houghton Mifflin Co., 1960.

Foerster, Norman. *American Criticism: A Study in Literary Theory from Poe to the Present.* Boston: Houston Mifflin Co., 1928.

Fuller, Margaret. "Modern British Poets." In *Art, Literature and the Drama.* Edited by Arthur B. Fuller. Boston: Brown, Laggard and Chasi, 1860.

Gray, H. D. *Emerson: A Statement of New England Transcendentalism.* Stanford: Stanford University, 1917.

Harrison, John S. *The Teachers of Emerson.* New York: Sturgis & Walton Co., 1910.

Hopkins, Vivian C. *Spires of Form: A Study of Emerson's Aesthetic Theory.* Cambridge: Harvard University Press, 1951.

Krutch, Joseph W. *Henry David Thoreau.* New York: William Sloane Associates, 1948.

Lowell, James Russell. "Wordsworth." In *The Writings of James Russell Lowell.* Boston: Houghton, Mifflin & Co., 1898–1899.

McDowell, Tremaine. *William Cullen Bryant.* American Writers Series. New York: American Book Co., 1935.

Matthiessen, F. O. *American Renaissance: Art and Expression in the Age of Emerson and Whitman.* New York: Oxford University Press, 1941.

Newton, Annabel. *Wordsworth in Early American Criticism.* Chicago: University of Chicago Press, 1928.

Peacock, Markham L., Jr. *The Critical Opinions of William Wordsworth.* Baltimore: Johns Hopkins Press, 1950.

Perry, Bliss. *Emerson Today*. Princeton: Princeton University Press, 1931.

Plato. *The Dialogues of Plato*. Translated by Benjamin Jowett. Oxford: Oxford University Press, 1892. 5 vols.

Plato. *The Works of Plato*. Edited and translated by Thomas Taylor. London: R. Wilks, 1804. 5 vols.

Power, Julia. *Shelley in America in the Nineteenth Century*. Lincoln, Nebraska: University of Nebraska Press, 1940.

Scott, Leonora C. *The Life and Letters of Christopher P. Cranch*. Boston: Houghton Mifflin Co., 1917.

Shelley, Percy Bysshe. *The Complete Works of Percy Bysshe Shelley*. Edited by Roger Ingpen and Walter E. Peck. New York: Charles Scribner's Sons, 1926–1930. 10 vols.

Shepard, Odell. *Henry Wadsworth Longfellow*. American Writers Series. New York: American Book Co., 1934.

Sidney, Sir Phillip. *The Complete Works of Sir Philip Sidney*. Edited by Albert Feuillerat. Cambridge: Cambridge University Press, 1923. 3 vols.

Spiller, Robert E. et al. *Literary History of the United States*. New York: The Macmillan Co., 1948. 1st. ed., 3 vols.

Thoreau, Henry. *Collected Poems of Henry Thoreau*. Edited by Carl Bode. Chicago: Packard & Co., 1943.

Thoreau, Henry. *The Heart of Thoreau's Journals*. Edited by Odell Shepard. Boston: Houghton Mifflin Co., 1906.

Thoreau, Henry. *The Journals of Henry D. Thoreau*. Edited by Bradford Torrey and Francis H. Allen. Boston: Houghton Mifflin Co., 1906. Reprinted 1949.

Waggoner, Hyatt H. *American Poets from the Puritans to the Present*. Boston: Houghton Mifflin Co., 1968.

Whicher, Stephen E. *Freedom and Fate: An Inner Life of Ralph Waldo Emerson*. Philadelphia: University of Pennsylvania Press, 1953.

Whitman, Walt. *Complete Prose Works*. Philadelphia: David McKay, 1892.

Whitman, Walt. *The Poetry and Prose of Walt Whitman*. Edited by Louis Untermeyer. New York: Simon & Schuster, 1949.

Willcock, Gladys D. and Walker, Alice, eds. *The Arte of English Poesie*. Cambridge: Harvard University Press, 1936.

Woodbury, Charles J., ed. *Talks with Ralph Waldo Emerson*. New York: The Baker and Taylor Co., 1890.

Wordsworth, William. *Preface to Lyrical Ballads: The Poetical Works of William Wordsworth*. Edited by E. De Selincourt. Oxford: Clarendon Press, 1944. 5 vols.

ARTICLES

Baker, Carlos. "Emerson and Jones Very." *New England Quarterly*, VII (March 1934), 90–99.
Beach, Joseph W. "Emerson and Evolution." *University of Toronto Quarterly*, III (July 1934), 474–497.
Clark, Harry H. "Emerson and Science." *Philological Quarterly*, X (July 1931), 224–260.
Falk, Robert P. "Emerson and Shakespeare." *PMLA*, LVI (March 1941), 532–543.
Flanagan, John T. "Emerson as a Critic of Fiction." *Philological Quarterly*, XV (January 1936), 30–45.
Foster, Charles H. "Emerson as American Scripture." *New England Quarterly*, XVI (March 1943), 91–105.
Garrod, H. W. "Emerson." *New England Quarterly*, III (January 1930), 1–24.
Gohdes, C. F. "Whitman and Emerson." *Sewannee Review*, XXXVII (January-March 1926) 79–93.
Gorely, Jean. "Emerson's Theory of Poetry." *Poetry Review*, XXII (July-August 1931), 263–273.
Gross, Seymour L. "Emerson and Poetry." *South Atlantic Quarterly*, LIV (January 1955), 82–94.
Moore, John B. "Emerson on Wordsworth." *PMLA*, XLI (March 1926), 179–192.
Moore, John B. "The Master of Whitman." *Studies in Philology*, XXIII (March 1926), 77–89.
O'Daniel, Therman B. "Emerson as a Literary Critic." *CLA Journal*, VII (1964), 21–43, 157–189, 246–276.
Pettigrew, Richard C. "Emerson and Milton." *American Literature*, III (March 1931), 45–59.
Sanborn, F. B. "The Emerson-Thoreau Correspondence." *Atlantic Monthly*, LXIX (May 1892), 557–596.
Sutcliffe, Emerson G. "Emerson's Theories of Literary Expression." *University of Illinois Studies in Language and Literature*, VIII (1923), 9–152.
Thompson, Frank T. "Emerson's Indebtedness to Coleridge." *Studies in Philology*, XXIII (January 1926), 55–76.

Index